Eyewitness
ANIMAL

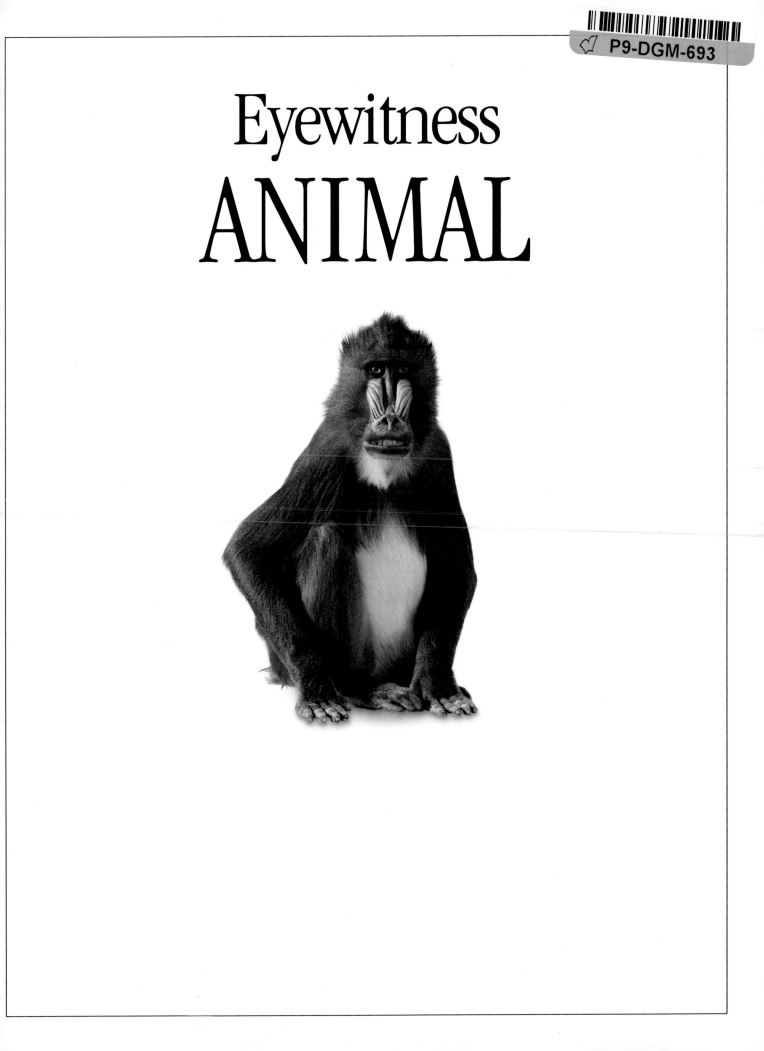

Totem pole featuring a thunderbird

Gold beetle

Tree skink with regenerating tail

Seal skeleton

Tarantula

Blue-footed boobies

China statuette of Lippizan dancing horse

Red-eyed
tree frog

Eyewitness
ANIMAL

Snake detecting
chemicals in air
with its tongue

Written by
TOM JACKSON

Common octopus

DK Publishing

Fisher's
lovebirds

European
common frog

LONDON, NEW YORK,
MELBOURNE, MUNICH, AND DELHI

Consultant Dr. Kim Dennis-Bryan

DK DELHI

Project editor Bharti Bedi
Project art editor Deep Shikha Walia
Senior editor Kingshuk Ghoshal
Senior art editor Govind Mittal
Senior DTP designer Tarun Sharma
DTP designer Neeraj Bhatia
DTP manager Sunil Sharma
Deputy managing editor Eman Chowdhary
Managing art editor Romi Chakraborty
Production manager Pankaj Sharma
Jacket designer Govind Mittal

DK LONDON

Senior editor Dr. Rob Houston
Senior art editor Philip Letsu
Publisher Andrew Macintyre
Picture researcher Myriam Mégharbi
Production editor Ben Marcus
Production controller Luca Frassinetti
US editor Margaret Parrish

Blue morpho
butterfly

Hamster

Homo habilis,
a human
ancestor

First published in the United States in 2012
by DK Publishing, 375 Hudson Street, New York, New York 10014

Copyright © 2012 Dorling Kindersley Limited, London

12 13 14 15 16 10 9 8 7 6 5 4 3 2 1

001—182469—Jul/12

A catalog record for this book is available from the Library of Congress.

ISBN 978-0-7566-9065-6 (Hardcover)
978-0-7566-9066-3 (Library binding)

Colour reproduction by MDP, UK
Printed and bound by Toppan Printing Co. (Shenzhen) Ltd., China

American
cockroaches

Penguin and chick

www.dk.com

Contents

What is an animal?

To date, only about 1 million of Earth's animal species have been identified. These range from a predatory tiger to dust-eating mites and even sea anemones and sponges—life-forms that many people don't think of as animals. Each of these animals is made up of millions, if not billions, of cells, which are specialized to perform different jobs in the body. Animals share the planet with plants, fungi, and many single-celled organisms. What sets animals apart from other many-celled organisms is that they are more mobile and survive by eating other life-forms.

BELONGING TO A SPECIES
The color, size, and body shape of this snake are among the traits that tell an expert that this is an emerald tree boa, a species that lives in the rainforests of South America. Every animal belongs to a species, the members of which look similar, follow the same kind of lifestyle, and live in the same habitats. Members of a species can breed with each other and produce young.

ANIMAL CELL
All living bodies are made up of tiny units called cells. Life-forms of each kingdom have their own set of cell features. An animal cell is surrounded by a membrane made from a thin sheet of oily material. The flexible membrane can take any shape—in contrast, plant cells have a fixed shape due to a rigid wall. Animal cells contain structures called organelles, which form the cell's factories (Golgi body), power supply (mitochondrion), and chemical transportation system.

Mitochondrion produces cell's energy

Nucleus houses cell's genes

Golgi body makes proteins

Liquid cytoplasm fills cell

GOING MOBILE
Animals are the only multicellular organisms (made from more than one cell) that can move from place to place as adults. Most plants are rooted to the ground and are not mobile. Locomotion is possible in animals because they do not have rigid body cells. This helps them alter their body shapes quickly, so they can push against the ground or water to move. Most plants can never change shape fast enough to carry themselves forward. Animals move in response to changes in their surroundings, generally to escape danger or to get nearer to food.

One line of symmetry divides animal into equal halves

Red-eared terrapin

Any vertical plane can divide animal into equal halves

Green sea anemone

DEVELOPMENT PLAN
Every animal grows from a single cell that divides repeatedly, developing into a body that can be made of billions of cells. Bodies of most animals, such as this terrapin, develop bilaterally, with a mouth at one end and vent (rear opening) at the other. Legs and all other body parts are divided equally between the left and right sides. Some simple animals, such as anemones, develop outward from a central point, producing circular bodies.

INSIDE THE ANIMAL KINGDOM
The ancient Greek philosopher Aristotle devised an early system of classification to organize the animal kingdom into groups, but this had some inaccuracies—dolphins were considered fish, for instance. The system used today was developed by the Swede Carl Linnaeus in the 1750s. He split the animal kingdom into a set of subgroups based on the shared features of the animals. Phylum is the largest subgroup, followed by class, order, family, genus, and then species. Every animal is described in terms of its position in each of these subgroups.

Classification of some salamander species

Chordata	(Phylum)
Vertebrata	(Subphylum)
Amphibia	(Class)

(Order): Caudata — Anura — Gymnophiona

(Family): Cryptobranchidae — Ambystomatidae — Plethodontidae — Sirenidae

(Genus): *Plethodon*

(Species): *jordani* — *cinereus* — *glutinosus*

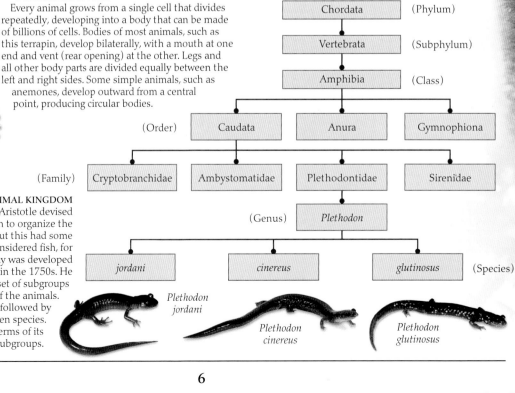

Plethodon jordani

Plethodon cinereus

Plethodon glutinosus

Ears and other sense organs tell the tiger about its surroundings

Bamboo is low on nutrients, so giant pandas eat it for as much as 16 hours a day

EATING FOOD

Of all the multicellular life-forms—plants, fungi, and animals—only animals eat. An animal eats food through its mouth. The body then extracts the nutrients it needs—the body's fuels and building materials—from the food and expels the rest as dung. In scientific terms, an animal is a heterotroph, meaning "other eater"—it survives by consuming the bodies of other life-forms. In contrast, a fungus grows into its food, absorbing nutrients through its body surface, while a plant is powered by the energy in sunlight and grows using raw materials absorbed from the ground through its roots.

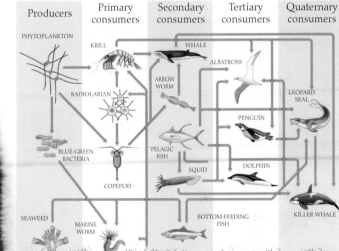

Producers | Primary consumers | Secondary consumers | Tertiary consumers | Quaternary consumers

PHYTOPLANKTON
KRILL
WHALE
ARROW WORM
ALBATROSS
RADIOLARIAN
LEOPARD SEAL
PENGUIN
BLUE-GREEN BACTERIA
PELAGIC FISH
COPEPOD
SQUID
DOLPHIN
SEAWEED
MARINE WORM
BOTTOM-FEEDING FISH
KILLER WHALE

WEBS OF FOOD

Most animals specialize in finding specific foods—which could be other animals. The animal community is, therefore, interconnected in networks, or food webs, that link everything edible in a habitat. This diagram shows a food web in the sea. It begins with producers, such as plants and bacteria—organisms that make their own food using energy from sunlight. Energy is then transferred to the primary consumers that feed on the producers, and so on. The arrows show the flow of energy.

Legs allow tiger to cross all types of land surfaces efficiently

ALMOST AN ANIMAL

Animals are not the only organisms to collect nutrients and fuel from other life-forms—fungi do the same, in their own way. Perhaps the closest life-forms to animals are a selection of microscopic organisms including amoebae—like the one seen above. These single-celled organisms can move to surround their tiny prey, such as algae, until it is completely engulfed.

Invertebrates

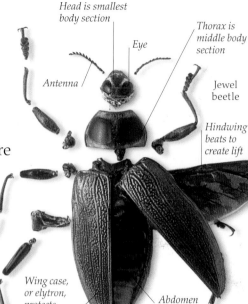

Head is smallest body section

Eye

Thorax is middle body section

Antenna

Jewel beetle

Hindwing beats to create lift

Wing case, or elytron, protects hind wing

Abdomen

Segment joins with others to make up leg

THE FIRST ANIMALS on Earth were invertebrates, which appeared in the oceans at least 700 million years ago. An invertebrate is an animal that does not have vertebrae, or spine bones. More than 95 percent of all animals are invertebrates. There are more than 20 totally different types, or phyla, such as arthropods (insects and relatives) and cnidarians (jellyfish, coral, and sea anemones). Lesser known invertebrates include organisms that are too small to see with the naked eye, such as dust mites, millions of which live in a house.

AS SIMPLE AS IT GETS
Invertebrates evolved from groups of single-celled organisms that teamed up to form simple multicellular bodies. Today's sponges may be similar to these first simple invertebrates. A sponge body works with just a handful of cell types. Pore cells let water into the body, and cone cells sieve food from it. Some cell types build the protein skeleton, including the spikes the sponge uses to fend off attack.

BLOOMING ANIMALS
Sea anemones are often mistaken for plants—they are even named after a type of flower—but they are carnivorous animals. Most invertebrates have one line of symmetry—one side of the body is a mirror image of the other—and they have a head at one end. However, anemones, jellyfish, and several other invertebrates have circular bodies, with no head at all.

Stinging tentacle can be mistaken for a petal

IN SECTIONS
There are at least 1 million species of insect, but these form only part of the world's biggest animal phylum—the arthropods. All arthropods have a segmented body, but in some, such as insects, some segments have fused (joined) during evolution to form body sections. Insect bodies are built in three sections—the head, thorax, and abdomen.

MANY MOLLUSKS
The mollusks form the second largest phylum of invertebrates, with 100,000 species. One species of mollusk can look totally different from another. Marine mollusks are often described as shellfish—people eat some of them, such as oysters and mussels. Snails are some of the most common land mollusks. All mollusk bodies have one muscular "foot" to move, and the organs are contained inside a fleshy mantle (a covering layer of tissue). Most mollusks have a protective shell strengthened with a chalky mineral called calcium carbonate. Several types, such as sea slugs, live without a shell.

Waterproof shell keeps body moist inside

Striped land snail

Mantle changes color, blending in with surroundings

Tentacle covered with suckers

MANY-FOOTED HEAD
The largest invertebrates of all are the cephalopods—a group of mollusks that includes octopuses, squid, and cuttlefish. A cephalopod's foot is divided into flexible tentacles—an octopus has eight, while some cephalopods have up to 90. Most of the body is the bulging mantle. This octopus has no shell, and there is only one hard body part—a hooked beak at the base of its tentacles.

Hard outer
skeleton is common
to all arthropods

Crayfish, an
arthropod

JOINTED FEET
Other than insects, the phylum
Arthropoda includes crustaceans
(lobsters and crabs), arachnids
(spiders and scorpions), and myriapods (centipedes
and millipedes). The name arthropod means "jointed foot,"
and all members of this group, including this crayfish, have
legs made from several hinged or coupled units. The
crayfish is an aquatic arthropod and breathes using
gills (see p.18). Most of those living on land breathe
using a network of tubes, or wind pipes, called
tracheae. These run throughout the body and
are connected to pairs of openings on the
body surface called spiracles, which let air in.

*Arm can
regenerate,
if lost*

Brittlestar, an
echinoderm

PLATES AND SPIKES
The echinoderms form a phylum of
sea invertebrates living on seabeds
everywhere, from seashore rock pools to
the deepest ocean trenches. Echinoderm
means "spiny skin." Many members of
this phylum, such as sea urchins, are
covered in sharp spikes. Others, such as
starfish and sea cucumbers, have hard
plates instead. None of them have
heads, while the mouth is in the
middle of the underside in most
cases. Most echinoderms
move very slowly by
pumping water into their
hundreds of pistonlike feet.

*Tentacle is sensitive
to taste and smell*

The bright colors
of neon sea slugs
warn predators
of toxins. This
alternative defence
suggests that the
mollusks can
afford to live
without a shell.

*Bristlelike
tentacle is
called chaeta*

Ragworm

A WORLD OF WORMS
Worms belong to several unrelated groups,
including three large phyla—the flatforms,
roundworms, and annelids (segmented
worms). Out of these, the largest worms are
the annelids, which include the earthworms,
leeches, and this ragworm, which lives on
the seabed. An annelid's body is made up
of segments joined in a chain, many times
over. Some annelids are among the longest
animals in the world, reaching a length of
more than 66 ft (20 m). Many roundworms,
or nematodes, are parasitic (see pp.46–47)
and live inside other animals. Many
flatworms are also parasites.

Cold-blooded vertebrates

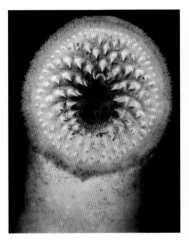

Eardrum is on the outside of the head

VERTEBRATES BELONG TO A PHYLUM called Chordata. All chordates have a notochord—a stiff rod running down the middle of their back. In vertebrates, this notochord has developed during evolution into a chain of bony segments, forming a backbone, or spine. Each spine bone is called a vertebra. Fish, amphibians, and reptiles are all ectothermic, or cold-blooded, vertebrates. Ectotherms cannot maintain a constant body temperature. Instead, their body temperatures depend on the temperature of their surroundings. Some ectothermic animals are sluggish in cold weather and need to warm up before they can move around actively.

Throat pouch is puffed up in males to make calls

Moist skin allows oxygen and water to pass through

NOT A VERTEBRATE
The lancelet is one example of a chordate that is not a vertebrate. It lives in the sea and grows to about the length of a person's finger. A lancelet has only a stiff chord supporting its back. It has no skull, limbs, or side fins. Biologists believe that vertebrates evolved from animals that looked like the lancelet, about 530 million years ago.

WITHOUT JAWS
Most vertebrates have jaws. Their mouths open and close using a bone hinged to the skull. However, this lamprey is jawless. It cannot bite its food. Instead, it twists its eel-like body to dig its spiral of teeth into the flesh of animals or to scrape food from rocks.

Tail carries a venomous sting

WITHOUT BONE
A vertebrate's body gets its shape because of a stiff internal skeleton. In most cases, the skeleton is made from bone—a honeycomb of cells that is strengthened with a mineral called calcium phosphate. However, many fish—such as sharks and these stingrays—have bones built of cartilage, which is made from protein. Their bones are more flexible than mineral bones.

RAYS OF BONE

Most fish have ray fins formed from scaly skin stretched over slim shafts, or rays, of bone. Ray fins are ideal for wafting water, but they are too weak to hold a fish's weight. Land vertebrates evolved from fish, but their legs did not develop from ray fins. Instead, lobe-finned fish, which have fleshy fins containing thick bones, are the ancestors of today's land vertebrates.

Large thigh muscle powers jump

Long leg has bones that lever frog forward

Pectoral fin used for balancing and braking

Tail, or caudal, fin used for propulsion

Frilly gill absorbs oxygen from water

LEADING LEAPER

The amphibians were the first land vertebrates. They are the ancestors of all existing tetrapods—animals with four limbs (including wings). Primitive tetrapods looked very different from today's most common amphibians—frogs. Frogs are built to jump. They have very long back legs, which are ideal for leaping into water and also help them hop on land. Like today's frogs, the primitive tetrapods had short, rigid necks and could not swivel their heads.

Webbed feet help in swimming

LIFE WITHOUT LEGS

Snakes have no legs at all. This makes it easier for them to slide through narrow burrows, twist and turn through tree branches, and slither over loose sand. Strong species, such as this cobra, can even rise up to stare into the eyes of taller animals. Snakes evolved from animals with legs. Some snake skeletons have hip bones, where legs once connected. Anacondas still have two tiny clawlike legs, which they use while mating.

BETWEEN TWO WORLDS

The word amphibian comes from the Greek word *amphibios* meaning "both lives." As a general rule, amphibians start their lives in water, hatching from eggs laid in pools. Young amphibians breathe with gills and swim with fins—like a fish. As they grow, they develop legs for moving on land and switch to lungs for breathing. However, some amphibian species mix up both ways of life. This mudpuppy stays underwater for its whole life but uses its legs to walk on the bottom of rivers and streams.

HIGH AND DRY

The reptiles were the first vertebrates to adopt a life away from water. Their eggs have a hard waterproof shell that prevents the eggs from drying out when laid. Reptilian scales also help waterproof the skin. This agama lizard will not dry out as it basks in the warm Sun. However, as reptiles are cold-blooded and cannot heat their bodies, most of them are restricted to living in warm parts of the world.

Wing-shaped pectoral fin flaps to propel ray forward

Warm-blooded vertebrates

BIRDS AND MAMMALS ARE THE ONLY endothermic, or warm-blooded, animals. Endothermic means "heat within." Endotherms can keep their body temperature constant, and, often, this means keeping the body warmer than the surroundings—using a blanket of fur, fat, or feathers to keep the heat in. Endotherms also use cooling systems, such as sweating or panting, during hot conditions. Water evaporates from the skin or tongue, helping cool the body. Thanks to their internal temperature controls, the bodies of endotherms can work well in most environments. As a result, they have spread to all parts of Earth—including the icy polar regions that are too cold for most other life-forms.

FLEXIBLE FEATHERS
A bird's plumage, or covering of feathers, has several functions. Fluffy down feathers grow close to the skin, trapping air pockets around the body. This air blanket stops heat from escaping. The large feathers are used for flight. They are long, stiff, and very lightweight. The feathers are also colored and camouflage the bird. In the case of this macaw, its coloring attracts mates.

Feathers overlap to form single flight surface

Quill has tiny barbs that make it painful to pull out when stuck in skin

FLIGHTLESS
The kiwi lives in New Zealand. This part of the world had no mammal predators, such as cats, until humans arrived 750 years ago. Since it had no need to fly, the kiwi did not develop a breastbone shaped to support strong flight muscles—making it a member of a group of flightless birds called ratites. It was safe on the ground, probing the soil for insects with its long beak.

Long flight feather extends backward from bone at front of wing

FEATHER VS HAIR
Reptile scales are coated in a waxy protein called keratin. Hair and feathers are also made of it, but instead of covering the skin, the keratin grows out of it in strands. Strands of mammal hair are of different lengths. The short underfur insulates, while longer guard hairs keep water and dirt away from the skin. Feathers are more complex than hair. The strands branch out from a central shaft, before dividing again to form a set of filaments that hook together into a flat surface. Water and dirt may easily cover the feathers, disrupting flight, so birds spend a large part of their day cleaning and maintaining their plumage.

PRICKLES AND TUFTS
Mammal hair is sometimes put to unusual uses. For example, the defensive spikes, or quills, of a porcupine are very thick hairs. When threatened, a porcupine raises its quills, making itself appear larger than it is. Most of the quills point backward, so if a predator attacks from behind, it will get a sharp shock. Porcupines may also behave aggresively, attacking predators and impaling them with the sharp quills. Other animals use hairs to communicate. Bushy-tailed squirrels have fluffy tails, which they flick to communicate with each other.

False-color electron micrograph of fox fur

False-color electron micrograph of dove feather

Porcupine quills

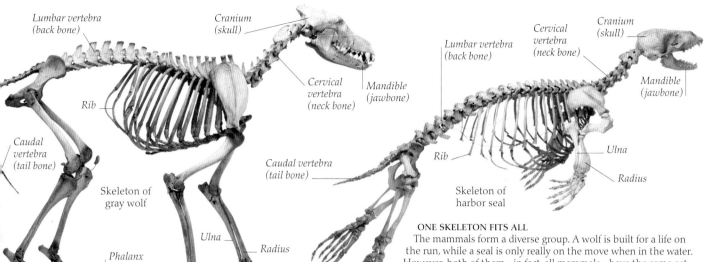

Lumbar vertebra
(back bone)

Cranium
(skull)

Cervical
vertebra
(neck bone)

Mandible
(jawbone)

Rib

Caudal
vertebra
(tail bone)

Skeleton of
gray wolf

Phalanx
(toe bone)

Ulna

Radius

Lumbar vertebra
(back bone)

Cervical
vertebra
(neck bone)

Cranium
(skull)

Mandible
(jawbone)

Rib

Caudal vertebra
(tail bone)

Ulna

Radius

Skeleton of
harbor seal

Phalanx
(toe bone)

ONE SKELETON FITS ALL

The mammals form a diverse group. A wolf is built for a life on the run, while a seal is only really on the move when in the water. However, both of them—in fact, all mammals—have the same set of bones. These bones differ from one mammal to another in terms of their relative sizes, among other things. The seal's flippers are long, flat versions of the wolf's springlike feet. Both animals have seven neck vertebrae—the same number as that of a human or a giraffe. A giraffe has no extra neck bones. The seven it has are just immensely long.

LAYING EGGS

When mammals first evolved from reptiles, about 200 million years ago, they all laid eggs. Today, most mammals give birth to live young. They make up two of the three kinds of mammals—placentals (those whose mothers nurture young inside their bodies with a placenta) and marsupials (those that give birth to immature young and nurture them inside a pouch). The duck-billed platypus does not belong to either. When it was first discovered, scientists were surprised to find that it laid eggs. The platypus is one of the five egg-laying mammal species, which together make up the third mammal group, called monotremes.

Long, colored
tail feather
attracts mates

Forward-facing eye

PRIMATES

This mandrill is a primate. The primates are examples of placental mammals and include monkeys, lemurs, and apes. Primates are one of the most widespread mammalian groups—humans are also primates and have spread to all parts of the globe. Primates evolved in the treetops, and the big brains they developed were useful in working out safe routes from branch to branch. Their forward-facing eyes provide precise binocular vision for judging distances. They climb using their long limbs and grasping hands.

Orca, or killer
whale, breaches
surface of water

MAMMALS IN WATER

Several mammal groups have evolved to survive in the water. Many such mammals—for instance, sea lions—still spend time on land. However, the cetaceans (whales and dolphins) never set foot on shore and do not even have feet. Instead of forelegs, they have flippers—and there are no hind limbs at all. The cetaceans are divided into two groups—the toothed whales, which include orcas and dolphins, and baleen whales, which include the blue whale. The blue whale is the largest living animal.

Evolution

Every species appears to be a perfect fit for its way of life. For example, a sea snake has a flattened, paddle-shaped tail that helps it swim, while a burrowing snake has a smooth, shovel-shaped snout suited to digging through soil. Both snakes have changed over time, evolving adaptations that better suit them to the environments in which they live. The driving force behind evolution is a process called natural selection. This is powered by the way animals must compete to survive and reproduce. Those better equipped to survive are more successful at breeding—and "selected" by nature. The weaker varieties perish. In this way, natural selection has shaped—and continues to shape—every species on Earth.

INHERITED FEATURES

Evolution is linked to the fact that animals inherit features from their parents. The instructions for making a body are contained in an animal's genes—a series of codes held on a chainlike chemical called deoxyribonucleic acid (DNA). This is present in every cell of an animal. DNA is passed to offspring, including any genes that give the parent animal an advantage or a disadvantage over others. Natural selection ensures that animals with advantageous genes flourish and have many offspring. As a result, their version of DNA becomes more common.

Thymine (T)

Guanine (G)

Adenine (A)

Cytosine (C)

A strand of DNA contains many copies of four chemical units, or bases. Genes are coded by strings of the bases A, C, T, and G.

DNA backbone contains molecules of sugar

Long, toothy snout helps snap up prey

Hind limb bone connects to pelvis (structure made of hip bones)

Tall vertebra anchors strong muscles supporting the head

Pakicetus evolved around 55 million years ago. It had hoofed feet but was a wolf-sized hunter, plunging into shallow water to catch fish.

Hoofed foot

BLIND PROGRESS

Evolution is happening all the time. The process has no direction—an animal can even seem to reverse its evolutionary path. For example, mammals evolved from animals whose ancestors were fish. These fish gradually developed walking legs from their pectoral and pelvic fins. Much later, some mammals again began pursuing a watery lifestyle. Their legs gradually evolved into finlike flippers, and their bodies became fish-shaped. The result was today's whales. On the left are four stages in this evolutionary process.

Powerful tail helps animal swim

Ambulocetus lived about 50 million years ago and hunted like a crocodile.

Legs used to swim in water and to walk on land

Feet are webbed

Jawbone picks up sounds like in modern whales

Body is 16 ft (5 m) long

Hind limb is a small flipper

Bones of hind limb are no longer attached to pelvis

Nostril is halfway along snout

Dorudon lived about 38 million years ago. It spent its life in warm seas eating fish and mollusks.

Tail is flattened into paddlelike flukes

Elongated skull helps crack through Arctic ice

Balaena, or the bowhead whale, is alive today. It has the largest mouth in the animal kingdom and filter-feeds on tiny krill (a type of crustacean).

Tiny hind limb bones

Forelimb is a flipper

THE FATHER OF EVOLUTION

In 1859, the English scientist Charles Darwin put forward the idea of evolution by natural selection in a book called *On the Origin of Species*. Darwin was influenced by the discoveries of Charles Lyell and others who showed that Earth was very old indeed—many millions of years—and had undergone many changes in that time. Later, scientists found more evidence to back up Darwin's theory. Francis Crick and James Watson showed how DNA coded genes, which are responsible for the inheritance of traits. This is crucial for evolution.

CO-EVOLUTION

In some cases, different organisms evolve together, in a process called co-evolution. These acacia ants have co-evolved with the bullhorn acacia shrub, with both species now highly adapted to life with the other. The ants make nests in the shrub's hollow thorns. They sting any herbivores that try to eat the plant's leaves, and they chew through any creepers that invade the branches. In return, the acacia provides the ants with sweet nectar and grows fatty nodules for them to eat.

Thorn is a small, sharp spine

Ants patrol the plant

NEVER THE SAME

Natural selection exists because no two animals are the same. Even members of the same species are at least slightly different because they have a unique set of genes. They may not look like it, but these two ladybugs belong to the same species. Their conspicuous patterns act as a warning to birds and other predators that the ladybugs taste nasty. Despite this, a bird may eat one of the ladybugs. The other one may survive successfully and produce offspring.

Azara's agouti lives on forest floors in South America. It collects fruits and roots.

The gray squirrel collects nuts from trees using its long tail for balance.

The Arabian spiny mouse searches for seeds among leaves and grasses.

RADIATING SPECIES

These rodents evolved from a single ancestor that lived 65 million years ago—shortly after the dinosaurs died out. When different descendants of a single species evolve in different directions, the result is called adaptive radiation. It gives rise to a whole range of new species that live in different habitats but share several features. For example, all rodents have long front teeth that can be used to gnaw tough plant foods.

SURVIVAL OF THE FITTEST

Darwin described animals with good genes that were able to survive and reproduce as being "fit." In these terms, a fit animal is not just strong and healthy like an athlete—its body and behavior make it successful at surviving and reproducing. This cheetah is "fit" because it has managed to get within pouncing distance of a wildebeest. However, the cat's victim is not "fit." It has not reacted to danger as fast as its herd mates and so is likely to be attacked.

Slow wildebeest allows cheetah to get too close

Extinct animals

IT MAY BE SURPRISING TO KNOW that 99 percent of all species to have lived on Earth are extinct. The animals that live today make up only 1 percent of life-forms that have existed in the course of Earth's history. Over the last 700 million years, the animal kingdom has constantly changed, with new species taking the place of older ones. A species becomes extinct when its remaining members fail to produce offspring. Extinction is a natural process. A species may die out when a new one evolves and outcompetes it in the struggle for survival. The new species may be better at finding food, or it may simply be a hunter that the old species has no defense against. Animals may also become extinct due to natural disasters. Whatever the reasons, all species eventually die out.

Echmatocrinus,
a primitive
echinoderm

STUDYING FOSSILS

Everything we know about extinct animals comes from fossils, which are the remains of animals, their footprints, and their droppings, preserved in rocks that may be millions of years old. It is rare for whole skeletons to be preserved. Paleontologists, or fossil scientists, build up a picture of how the animal looked and lived from fragments of bone, often comparing them to those of modern animals. For example, the large eye of this icthyosaur—an extinct sea reptile—shows that it dived into dark waters. The long toothy snout suggests that it preyed on slippery fish.

AN EXPLOSION OF LIFE

No one knows if all animals evolved from a common ancestor. What we do know is that almost all animals living today—from fish to fleas—had an ancestor that was swimming in the ocean during the Cambrian period. This was because a great blooming of species—called the Cambrian Explosion—happened around 530 million years ago (mya). All of the Cambrian species, including the invertebrates seen here, are now extinct, but they paved the way for the animal diversity we see today.

Opabinia
(possibly a
giant ancestor
of a tardigrade)

Haikouichthys,
one of the
earliest
vertebrates

Marrella
(thought to be a
primitive arthropod)

MASS EXTINCTIONS

Extinctions may occur due to a global catastrophe that wipes out thousands of species all at once. Earth has witnessed at least five mass extinctions, the last of which occurred 65 mya when the dinosaurs died out suddenly. Scientists think that a huge asteroid hitting Earth at that time, combined with an increase in erupting volcanos, made it impossible for many life-forms to survive. The worst extinction of all was the one around 250 mya, which wiped out most life on Earth.

Corythosaurus, a dinosaur

Plates of armor on trilobite's back allowed the creature to roll up for protection

EXTINCT HUMANS

Our species, *Homo sapiens,* is not the first species of human being. It is just the only one that has not died out yet. One of the earliest members of the *Homo* genus was *Homo habilis,* which lived between 2.3 and 1.4 mya. *Homo habilis* means "handy man." Paleontologists have identified a dozen other human species as well. The last one to become extinct was the 3½-ft-(1-m-) tall "Flores man"—*Homo floresiensis*—which died out about 17,000 years ago.

Homo habilis made cutting tools out of flakes of stone

KILLED BY HUMANS

The thylacine, or marsupial tiger, became extinct in 1936 when the last one died in an Australian zoo. By then, all wild thylacines—predators more closely related to kangaroos than cats—had been shot, as they were considered pests. Humans have wiped out hundreds of other species—often by accident. One of the earliest known cases was the Cuban coney, a rodent that was hunted to extinction by dogs. The dogs were introduced to Cuba by humans who settled on the Caribbean island soon after it was discovered by Christopher Columbus in 1493.

DEAD END

An extinct species often leaves behind sister species. For example, the dinosaurs were survived by relatives such as crocodiles and birds. But some extinctions spell the end for an entire group of animals. Trilobites, for instance, used to be one of the most common animals in the sea before they were all wiped out in the mass extinction around 250 mya.

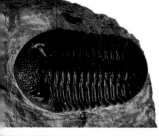

Anomalocaris, a primitive arthropod

Hallucigenia (possibly a velvet worm)

Wiwaxia, a primitive annelid

Body systems

AN ANIMAL'S BODY IS A MACHINE. For an animal to stay alive, its body must be supplied with fuel and raw materials. The body must also get rid of waste and repair itself when damaged. To carry out these functions and many more, the body of most animals is divided into a series of systems, each devoted to one set of life processes. Animals of all types use the same basic set of body systems, which process food, distribute raw materials, manage movements, and protect the body. Bodies of different animals perform the same jobs in different ways. An octopus pumps blood with three hearts, while birds, unlike humans, never produce liquid urine—their waste mostly comes out as white droppings.

Hard wing case covers beetle's back

SKELETONS
Rigid skeletons provide a framework to an animal's body. In the case of land animals, this allows the organisms to raise their body parts against the pull of gravity. More importantly, the skeleton provides anchor points for muscles to pull on, which allows animals to move their body parts and to move from place to place. A vertebrate has an internal skeleton made of bones or cartilage, but an insect, such as this beetle, has an exoskeleton (skeleton outside the body) made from a tough material called chitin. This exoskeleton defines the animal's shape.

THE FLOW OF BLOOD
Blood is made of cells, which carry oxygen, floating in water mixed with a range of chemicals. The chemicals include hormones—chemical messengers that control different body systems. These systems are fed by blood vessels that form the main chemical transport network of a living body, in the case of most animals. Blood vessels are always inside an animal's body, but can be seen through the thin skin of some animals, such as this glass frog. Invertebrates do not have blood vessels. Instead, the blood sloshes through the whole body. An animal's body parts would begin to die without a supply of blood and the oxygen it contains.

Heart pumps blood around body

Crab spider sucks out digested insides of its prey

FLESHY SOUP
Usually, after swallowing food, an animal must digest it, or break it down, into the basic ingredients—sugars, fats, and proteins. It then uses these substances as fuel or to build up the body. Most of the digestion is done by powerful chemicals in the stomach and intestines called enzymes. A spider digests its food a little differently, though. It does not chew its food. Instead, it pumps its stomach enzymes into its prey, turning the victim's insides into a fleshy soup, which the spider then sucks up.

Pouch around gill is full of water so gill works even if animal is above water

GAS EXCHANGE
Animals must take in oxygen and give out carbon dioxide, a process called gas exchange. Oxygen burns—or chemically processes—sugar, releasing energy, and producing carbon dioxide as waste. While simple animals can exchange gases through the surface of their body, larger creatures use more efficient systems like lungs and gills to bring the blood into close contact with the oxygen supply. This mudskipper's gills take oxygen from water—even when the fish crawls into the air.

Body organs seen
through the belly
of a glass frog

BRAIN CHAIN

The body's main communication
system is made up of nerves, which work
as wires carrying electric signals. The nerves
connect to junction boxes—each of which is
called a ganglion. The ganglia (plural of ganglion)
take care of different body sections. Vertebrates have a
centralized nervous system, with all ganglia and nerves under
the control of the brain. Insects, such as this cockroach,
instead have a chain of nearly independent ganglia.
The cockroach can survive for some time even
if its head—carrying the brain—is cut off.

*Nerve
connects
to muscles*

*Ganglion controls
movement, even
when head is cut off*

*Body shortens
because longitudinal
muscles contract*

Leech pulled
into a ball

*Body begins to
lengthen as circular
muscles contract*

Leech extends
its head

*Body flattens
as longitudinal
muscles relax*

*Sucker
anchors body*

Narrow
body is
fully
stretched

PULL AND STRETCH

Animals move using muscles, which are built up from tiny
fibers made of two types of protein—actin and myosin.
When the fibers receive an electric pulse from a nerve, one
protein hauls itself along the other, causing the fiber to
shorten, or contract. A contracting muscle pulls on the
body, changing its shape—such as drawing this leech into
a ball. However, muscles cannot push, so they work
in paired groups in which one set produces the opposite
movement to the other and vice versa, in sequence.

*Translucent
skin covers
belly*

*Vein carries blood
back to heart*

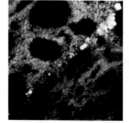

The blue skin of this
frog warns predators
that it is poisonous

Tiger stripes help
the cat hide in
dry grasses

CLEVER SKIN

Skin is an animal's main contact with the
outside world. It is a tough barrier but also
a highly sensitive one, alerting the animal
to cold, heat, and the slightest touch. It is
also a self-repairing structure that acts as
the first line of defense against diseases.
Skin takes many forms, often buried
beneath protective insulation, such as a
mammal's hair or a bird's feathers. Reptiles
have scales waterproofed by keratin, while
frog skin is very much a two-way body
covering—allowing water, oxygen, and
chemicals to move through it easily.

Crocodile scales are
armored with
plates of bone

A parrot's
bright plumage
attracts mates

Sharp senses

IN ORDER TO SURVIVE, an animal needs to gather information about its surroundings. It must search for its meals, look out for threatening predators, and find a member of its own species to mate with. An animal uses its senses for these purposes. Each type of sense builds up an impression of the area around the animal using a certain kind of clue, such as light, pressure, heat, or chemicals. To hear a sound, for instance, the ear collects pressure waves traveling through the air. An animal uses such information to make split-second decisions that could make the difference between life and death.

ALL EYES
The tarsier is a relative of monkeys, with a body no bigger than a person's hand. However, a tarsier's eyes are huge, taking up more room in its head than the brain. The tarsier hunts for insects at night and needs big eyes to collect enough light to see—in the same way as astronomers use wide-lens telescopes to see faint stars.

Middle band is a specialized color detector

Each eye has 10,000 lenses

SPACE DETECTORS
When a mouse searches for food in total darkness, it relies on its sense of touch to move around safely. Vibrassa, or special whiskers, are touch-sensitive hairs that stick out from its snout. If the vibrassa fit through a space without being bent or blocked too much, a mouse can be sure that the rest of the body will also fit through.

MULTICOLORED WORLD
Eyes detect light using chemicals called pigments. Each pigment triggers an electric pulse when hit by a ray of light. The pulse travels along nerves to the brain, which builds a picture from many pulses. The most complex eyes belong to the mantis shrimp. Its eye has 12 pigments, compared to only three in the human eye. Each pigment is sensitive to a different color. Mantis shrimp not only can detect the whole rainbow of colors, but can also see heat and ultraviolet light, both invisible to humans. It uses its ultrasensitive eyes to identify its favorite coral foods—and even find mates by the way they glow.

DISH FACE
An owl is a silent hunter. Its wings make no noise as it swoops in for a kill. The owl tracks sounds from voles and other animals to carefully target its prey before attacks. The faint sounds are collected by the disk of feathers around the face, which works like a satellite dish picking up signals from space. The facial disk focuses the sound into the owl's ears beneath the feathers.

Prey

Jelly inside an ampulla converts electric signals into nerve pulses

Nerve carries pulses to brain

Faint electric field produced by fish's muscles

SCANNER SYSTEM
Like many fish, sharks can feel the movements created in water when animals swim past. Sharks are also sensitive to electric signals produced by their prey. Muscle movement in prey animals forms weak electric fields that surround the shark's victims in the water. These signals are picked up by tiny pits, called ampullae of Lorenzini, dotted around the shark's snout. The ampullae even allow sharks to scan for prey buried in sand.

Feather-shaped antenna traps chemicals floating in the air

Pointed tip of the tongue collects scent chemicals in the air

Micrographs of jewel beetle and its fire detectors

HOT SPOTTERS
Most animals get away from forest fires as fast as they can. However, the fire-detecting beetle flies straight for them. The beetle looks for recently burned trees to make suitable homes for its wood-eating grubs. The insect finds the fire using an array of tiny heat sensors located behind its second pair of legs. The sensors are sensitive enough to pinpoint a fire from 7.5 miles (12 km) away.

SCENT FEELERS
Antennae, the appendages on an invertebrate's head, are generally used to feel objects. However, male moths use these feathery antennae more often to sweep the air for smells. The moth is most interested in picking up pheromones—special scent chemicals—released by the females. Some moth species can smell a mate from 6 miles (10 km) away.

TASTING THE AIR
Snakes are hunters, and most of them rely on their sense of smell to find food. However, in addition to sniffing the air, a snake tastes it by flicking out its long tongue. The snake then slots the forked tips of the tongue into a scent detector—known as the Jacobson's organ—on the roof of its mouxth. If one tongue tip has more scent on it than the other, the source of the smell must be in that direction.

Animal diets

MULTICELLULAR LIFE FORMS ARE POWERED in different ways—a plant gets its energy from sunlight, while a fungus digests its food by growing into it, and an animal collects food and takes it into its body. Diet is a deciding factor in what an animal looks like and how it survives. Some species are tuned to exploit one food source, while others survive on whatever comes their way. For instance, the snail kite is a little predatory bird that swoops over South American marshlands to prey only on snails. Away from the marshland, the kite would starve. In contrast, the Andean condor is an immense bird that glides for miles in search of a meal. It is ready to eat anything, from the carcass of a beached whale to a nest full of eggs.

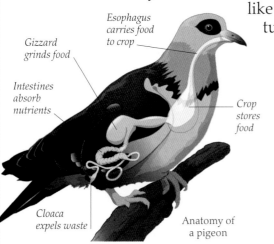

Gizzard grinds food

Esophagus carries food to crop

Intestines absorb nutrients

Crop stores food

Cloaca expels waste

Anatomy of a pigeon

Long neck helps giraffe reach fresh leaves that most browsers cannot reach

DIGESTING SEEDS
Many small birds, such as pigeons, are seed eaters. Seeds are packed with energy, which powers the growth of new plants. However, most seeds also have hard kernels, and birds have no teeth and so cannot chew. Instead, a muscular stomach pouch called the gizzard grinds the seeds against one another, helping release all the seed's valuable nutrients. Some birds even peck up specks of grit to help grind the seeds more efficiently.

THE ULTIMATE BROWSER
The giraffe is the ultimate browser—an animal that eats leaves. It twists its tough, long tongue around branches to strip away leaves, even from the prickliest trees. Browsers and grazers (animals that eat grasses) are herbivores and eat only plant food. Leaves and bark in particular lack nutrients—most of this diet is indigestible fiber. Plants fend off animal attacks by producing chemicals, called tannins, which make leaves even harder to digest. Therefore, herbivores must feed constantly to keep their bodies supplied with energy. Like many large herbivores, the giraffe relies on stomach bacteria to break down some of the fiber into useful sugars.

SEEK AND DESTROY
Animals that eat nothing but meat are known as carnivores. A diet of flesh is very nutritious. It is packed with energy and full of the proteins and fats needed to build a strong body. However, to maintain a supply of fresh meat, a carnivore must use a lot of energy to catch prey. This lioness is running after a meal, while its prey—a kudu calf—is running for its life. Even a predator as strong and as fast as a lioness fails to kill in six out of seven hunts.

COOPERATIVE FARMERS

Leaf-cutter ants grow their own food. Thousands of them live in underground nests. Worker ants use their slicing mouthparts to cut slabs of leaves from the surrounding trees. The ants then carry the leaves back to the nest and pile them up in deep "garden" chambers. A species of fungus grows on the heaps of rotting leaves and that is what the adult ants eat and feed to their young. Like any good farmer, these ants tend their crops, applying pesticide chemicals in their saliva to stop the fungus from becoming infected with bacteria.

Leaves of the acacia tree are clustered at the top, beyond the reach of most browsers

Dung of herbivores, such as cattle, is preferred by the beetles

Long back leg used to roll dung

EVERYTHING IS FOOD

Herbivores can only extract a small proportion of nutrients from their food—60 percent of an elephant's food is barely digested at all—and so the feces, or dung, that leaves their bodies is a useful source of food for other animals. A dung beetle collects such waste by rolling it into balls, inside which they lay their eggs. When the grubs hatch, they have a ready-made supply of dung to feast on.

Head feathers are short so they do not get soaked with blood from carcasses

FLESH OF THE DEAD

Animals that eat carrion—the flesh of dead animals—are called scavengers. Top scavengers include vultures, which patrol the skies on their wide wings. A vulture spirals down to any dead body it spots with its acute eyesight. A vulture's hooked beak is ideal for ripping scraps of flesh from bones. The bird's stomach juices are extremely acidic. This kills any dangerous bacteria that may have infected the rotting carcasses.

Rüppell's vulture

CURIOSITY PAYS

Some animals never miss a chance to eat a meal. Such opportunist feeders are generally omnivores—animals that eat plant and animal food, dead or alive. The coati, a raccoonlike opportunist in South America, searches everywhere for food, sniffing it out with a long nose. It checks every nook and cranny with its sensitive forepaws. The coati's curiosity means it can find food almost anywhere—from a jungle to a junk yard.

Breeding and young

AN ANIMAL THAT DIES without reproducing cannot pass on its genes. The animal, and its genes, becomes extinct. In nature, the only types of animal that survive are those that are driven to reproduce. The simplest method is just to split in half, or allow offspring to bud off. Budding is a type of asexual reproduction—with only one parent. However, most animals use sexual reproduction, in which a male and female pair up. This mixes up the characteristics of the parents, increasing the chances that some offspring will survive. Animals often choose mates in complex courtships that show off their partner's strength. After hatching or being born, all young animals go through a period of growth. They may be supported by their parents or left to mature on their own.

Female   Male

COURTING A MATE
Strong and healthy animals make the best mates because it is likely that their offspring will be healthy, too. Most animals spend a lot of time choosing a mate. The male blue-footed booby puts on a show for a potential mate by spreading his wings and stamping his feet. The deep blue feet are a sign that this male might make a good mate. The female needs to be sure about the male she mates with since she will stay with him for life.

CHANGING SEX
Sexual reproduction requires a male sex cell (sperm) to fuse with a female one (ovum, or egg). Generally, an animal is either male or female—it produces sex cells of only one kind. However, a hermaphrodite animal, such as a snail, produces both kinds of cells at the same time. The bluehead wrasse is also a hermaphrodite, but changes sex from female to male. A young female normally lives with other females and a large, mature "supermale" that has a bright blue head. When this male dies, the largest adult female in the group changes sex to become the next supermale, producing sperm instead of eggs.

Young female does not have a blue head

Supermale has a blue head

PRECIOUS CARGO
It is not enough just to produce young. An animal needs to ensure that its offspring will survive long enough to reproduce themselves. Most invertebrates lay eggs in large numbers so that at least a few of the young survive to become adults. Scorpions, however, produce only a few eggs. The eggs hatch inside the mother, and the babies feed inside her body before being born. The young ones spend the first part of their lives on their mother's back. The mother protects her newborns so that they will have a better chance of growing up and breeding.

MOTHERED BY FATHER
Seahorses have a unique breeding system in which the males carry the eggs and give "birth." The female produces the eggs and transfers them to a brood pouch on the male's belly. The eggs hatch inside the pouch, but the young, called fry, do not leave it immediately. The pouch supplies the fry with oxygen and gradually increases in saltiness to prepare them for life in the sea water.

STARTER HOME
Most mammal babies develop inside their mother's womb, or uterus, where a structure called the placenta supplies them with oxygen and food until they are big enough to survive in the outside world. The placenta is absent or not well developed in marsupial mammals, such as this kangaroo, which give birth to immature offspring. The kangaroo's offspring is called a joey, and when it was born, it was blind and hairless and its hind legs were just little lumps. It had clawlike arms, which it used to heave itself into its mother's pouch. The pouch protects the joey and allows it to complete its development.

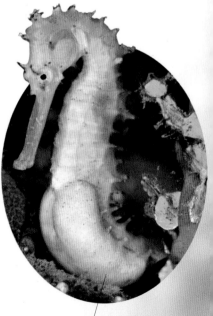

Pouch contains around 200 fry

Embryo inside jelly

Tail used for swimming

Gills

Newly hatched tadpole

Female aphid giving birth to young

Frog spawn

THE CYCLE OF LIFE

A frog goes through several stages during its life. After hatching from eggs, the young—or larvae—begin to grow in water. In the adult stage, the frog devotes its energy to finding a mate and producing eggs of its own. This takes place mainly on land. Since the adults are on land and larvae in water, they do not compete with each other for food. Much like frogs, many insects also have a life cycle divided into stages. The process of change from a larval to an adult stage—such as a caterpillar becoming a butterfly—is known as metamorphosis.

Half-tadpole, half-frog, 6–9 weeks

MASS REPRODUCTION

Populations of aphids—also known as greenfly—grow very quickly using a form of asexual reproduction known as parthenogenesis. Females give birth to tiny clones (identical versions of themselves). Even as they are born, these young aphids already have their own young developing inside them. In one summer alone, there can be 40 generations of aphid, resulting in thousands of these sucking insects on one plant. Parthenogenesis produces huge numbers quickly, but if one aphid has a weakness—a susceptibility to disease, for example—then every aphid will have it too. Therefore, in fall, aphids lay eggs using sexual reproduction that mixes up their genes, ensuring that a wide variety of aphids will hatch out in the next spring.

Adult common frog

Froglet emerges from water after about 12 weeks

Tail gradually shrinks

Front legs now fully formed

CARING PARENTS

Animals ensure the survival of their offspring in contrasting ways. Some animals, such as most invertebrates and many fish, produce many offspring and provide little parental care, while others, such as many mammals, have few young and devote a lot of time and energy to caring for them. Orangutans have one baby at a time, several years apart. The baby ape is almost helpless at birth. Its mother carries it through the trees for several months. It also has a lot to learn—how to climb and where to find food—and needs its mother's help for the first five years or so.

Female orangutan with her babies

Marine animals

LIFE BEGAN IN THE OCEANS more than
3.5 billion years ago, and the oceans are still
home to every major type of animal. However,
the oceans are not a single habitat. Marine environments
are as different as rocky shores, mangrove swamps, and deep
ocean trenches. Even in the open ocean, there are variations in
temperature, pressure, and saltiness that impact on what lives
there. The open ocean is on average 2.5 miles (4 km) deep,
and animals live at all depths. Living deep down means
coping with the dark—sea water absorbs sunlight
and no light ever penetrates deeper than about
3,300 ft (1,000 m). The pressure is also a lot
higher at depth, but this doesn't pose much
of a problem to the animals that live in the
deeps. Biologists estimate that there is
300 times more living space in Earth's
oceans than on dry land and there
must be animals out there that
are still unknown
to science.

PATROLLING THE SHORE
The shoreline is one of the most
crowded parts of the ocean. Here, the
tides sweep regularly over the shore
before receding. Covered by sea water
one minute and then being exposed to
the air the next is a challenge for coastal
animals. When the tide recedes, many
of them hide out in mud and sand flats
until the water rushes back over them.
These animals make up a rich source
of food for shorebirds, such as these
red knots, which raid the shore at low
tide to dig out shellfish and other prey.

COASTAL RAIDERS
Many sea mammals and birds live on the coast but
raid the water for food. Terns snatch fish, seals chase
down squid, and diving otters collect shellfish. The
sea otters have highly buoyant bodies. This is partly
because they have some of the thickest fur in the
animal kingdom, with 1 million strands per sq in
(150,000 strands of hair per sq cm), which traps lots of
air. These hunters float high in the water easily and can
lie on their backs while cracking open shells with a stone.
The otters can even sleep while bobbing at the surface.

UNDERWATER JUNGLES
Corals are colonies of organisms that are
tiny relatives of jellyfish. Each animal is called a
polyp and grows a tiny protective case made from
calcium carbonate, which is left behind when it dies.
Generations of these skeletons—some round, others in
plates or branches—build up into limestone reefs that can
be several miles long. It is the complex shapes, holes,
and crevices created by the coral skeletons that is the
main secret to the reef's richness—like a jungle,
it has a lot of different niches for animals, such
as these yellow butterflyfish, to live in.

SCHOOLING

There are few places to hide in the open ocean and some fish have to stick together to stay safe from predators. They do so by swimming in clusters called schools, or shoals. Small fish forming a school dart around, making it difficult for a predator to pick out a single target. Each fish seen here is trying to get into the middle of a shoal where it is safer, exposing those on the edges to potential predators that may be lurking around.

Spotted skin camouflages shark against seabed while it rests

A DOCILE SHARK

There are about 350 species of shark in the ocean. Some are fearsome, long-toothed predators that can easily prey on humans, but most sharks are quite harmless. This bullhead shark is about as long as a person's arm. It uses its sturdy fins to walk across the seabed at night, searching for urchins and crabs to feed on. The shark's teeth are flat and they simply crush its food.

Mantle (body covering)

Fin flaps up and down to push squid along

DEVIL IN THE DARK

The deep-sea vampire squid spends its life in constant darkness. It produces light from its own body—a phenomenon called bioluminescence. Chemical reactions in its skin produce light, which the squid flashes to lure prey and attract mates. If the squid's light brings unwanted attention from a predator, it folds its webbed tentacles over the mantle, shutting out the light in an instant.

Webbed tentacle

GOING FLAT

Flatfish, such as this flounder, go through an incredible transformation so they can lie flat on the seabed, ready to snap up worms and shrimps. A young flounder swims upright like other fish, but as the fish grows, its skull twists so that the right eye moves to the left side of the head. This way both the eyes are on the same side of the head and the fish can look for its prey while lying camouflaged on the seabed.

Freshwater living

White plumage turned pink by chemicals in diet

Thick skin is resistant to chemicals in water

MINERAL-RICH
Not every inland body of water contains fresh water. Flamingos live in desert lakes filled with salts and other chemicals, where no plants grow. Most water animals would die in these lakes. The flamingos survive by feeding on tough brine shrimps, which live on a diet of bacteria (small single-celled organisms).

Beak has plates that sift food from water

INLAND WATER HABITATS can be as challenging to life as the oceans. Fresh water contains little salt, while animal body tissues are full of salts, which pull water into the animals' bodies in a process called osmosis. Freshwater animals must produce watery urine constantly to flush it out. Many aquatic animals rely on unpredictable little streams and ponds, which may freeze in winter and dry out in summer. Some animals escape to larger ponds or rivers, but brine shrimps and tardigrades wait out dry periods as watertight eggs or dormant (inactive) forms. As water levels change in rivers, so does the current. Some fish in fast hill streams cling to rocks with suckerlike fins. Slow-flowing water loses oxygen and its fish cannot use their gills effectively, so some cope by taking gulps of air into lunglike sacs.

Bony scute protects body

LURKING IN THE SHALLOWS
Since crocodiles evolved around 240 million years ago, they have seen many impressive relatives—such as the dinosaurs—come and go. This spectacled caiman, like other crocodilians, is superbly suited to hunting in shallow waters. It lies hidden under the water with only the eyes and nostrils above the surface, ready to surge up the bank to drag prey into the water. This caiman also feeds on large quantities of fish. A crocodile's bite is 10 times stronger than that of a shark and once its victim is in the water, death by drowning or dismemberment (being torn apart) is almost certain.

ON THEIR OWN
Freshwater lakes are isolated habitats with unique wildlife in much the same way as remote islands far out at sea. Lake Baikal, the world's largest lake, in eastern Russia, is about 1,240 miles (2,000 km) from the Arctic Ocean. It is home to the only freshwater species of seal, known as the nerpa. The ancestors of the nerpa probably swam up river to the area about 80,000 years ago when the lake was much larger. Now the nerpa is a landlocked species, without a route back to the sea. The nerpa feed on spiny fish called sculpins.

Spider falls into water after getting hit by stream

SURVIVORS

Tardigrades, or water bears, are microscopic animals that live in all types of water—from hot springs to muddy puddles—and graze on bacteria. They were discovered in 1773 after biologists began using microscopes. Tardigrades are the toughest creatures known to exist. When the water in a tardigrade's habitat dries out or becomes too salty, it hauls up its eight legs and becomes dormant. Scientists have found that tardigrades can survive in almost any environment—even the vacuum of space.

Shot can be stream or droplets

TREE PONDS

Freshwater habitats can be found in some unusual places. The leaves of succulent jungle plants called bromeliads form a cup that collects rainwater. These little ponds, high up in the trees, are used by many poison dart frogs to raise their young. The mother lays a single egg, from which a tadpole hatches. She frequently checks up on the tadpole, laying unfertilized eggs in the water for it to eat or bringing it insects. If the baby outgrows its pool, the mother carries it to a larger one.

Eel swims by waving body from side to side

WATER CANNON

The archerfish uses water as a weapon. The fish positions itself with its lips poking out of the water. It then fires a jet of water out of its mouth with a quick squeeze of its gill covers. The jets of water can travel up to 10 ft (3 m) into the air, knocking invertebrate prey from overhanging leaves. The fish gobbles up its victims as they struggle in the water. Unlike other creatures that would see the prey out of position due to refraction, the archerfish mostly hits its target at the first attempt because its eyes and brain adjust to the refracted light. Refraction is the bending of light that happens when it moves from air to water.

A WATERY ROAD

Most aquatic (water-living) animals are adapted to one habitat. But this is not the case with the common eel—it has specialized kidneys that enable it to live in both salty and fresh water. This snake-shaped fish starts life in the Sargasso Sea and begins one of nature's most epic journeys—across the Atlantic Ocean and into the freshwater habitats in Europe and back. Baby eels, or elvers, head for river mouths, where fresh water mixes with salty sea water. Some elvers stay in these brackish (slightly salty) habitats, hiding from threats by burrowing in sand. Most elvers head inland, even slithering over land to reach a suitable freshwater habitat. Once mature, the adult eels head back to sea to breed.

Hawker naiad spears a stickleback fish

WET NURSERY

Very few insect species live in marine habitats, but many, such as the hawker dragonfly, start life in fresh water before emerging as adults on dry land. This young dragonfly—known as a naiad—has not yet developed the wings it will use as an adult. It breathes with gills and uses a sharp mouthpart to spear prey with lightning speed. After several months of hunting in shallow pools, the naiad climbs up the stalk of a water plant to transform into an adult. After the adult females have mated, they lay eggs at or near the water surface.

Cold and ice

THE COLDEST HABITATS on Earth are near the Poles, where summers are too short to provide much warmth, and high up on mountains, where the air is too thin to retain heat. Most of the animals that live in cold places tend to be endothermic, or warm-blooded. A few cold-blooded species have evolved adaptations that enable them to survive in cold conditions. The adders that live in cold regions are black. The dark scales of these snakes absorb heat better than their paler cousins that live in warmer climates. Meanwhile, in the mountains of New Zealand, the alpine wet, a large cricket, spends the winter frozen—but is still alive and well when it thaws out in spring.

BIGGER IS BETTER

In 1847, the German zoologist Christian Bergmann put forward a principle, now known as Bergmann's rule. It states that animals in cold regions are bigger than those in warm areas. Bodies of large animals lose heat slowly in cold conditions. The world's largest deer, the moose, lives in the cold north, as does the musk ox, the largest goat, and the gyrfalcon, the biggest falcon. In 1877, biologist Joel Asaph Allen came up with another principle (called Allen's rule). This stated that polar animals have shorter legs, ears, and tails, which also help reduce heat loss.

FOUND IN PLENTY

The polar oceans are so cold that the surface of the water freezes over at times. The conditions in the oceans are, however, less severe than on land. The polar seas thrive with life. The most abundant inhabitants of these waters are krill—tiny pink relatives of shrimp that live in swarms numbering millions of individuals. Krill are an important food source for blue whales and many other sea creatures.

Antarctic krill

LIFE IN THE ARCTIC

Earth's polar regions experience extreme seasonal changes. While it is totally dark for much of the winter, the Sun does not set for weeks on end during summer. Most polar bears are active throughout the year, but pregnant females enter a hibernation-like state and sleep through the winter. Bear cubs are born at this time, growing strong on their mother's milk while she is still asleep in the den. Mother and cubs are ready to hunt as soon as summer arrives.

Pale fur helps bear stay hidden among the ice

Wide feet do not sink into snow and make good paddles when swimming

HIGH FLIERS

Bar-headed geese cross over the Himalayas while migrating from the wetlands in India to the Tibetan plateau. These birds have been seen flying at heights of 33,382 ft (10,175 m)—higher than any other bird. Up there, pushed along by high winds, the geese can fly at a speed of around 150 mph (240 kph). The temperature at such great heights is -22°F (-30°C), and the air is so thin that the geese breathe hundreds of times in a minute to get enough oxygen.

Wings are larger than those of other geese

HAPPY FEET

Body heat can cause problems in freezing conditions. Warm skin melts ice but ice freezes again almost instantly, bonding to the skin in the same way that a tongue sticks to a cold ice lolly. Amazingly, penguins don't have to deal with this problem. Emperor penguins survive at -76°F (-60°C), the coldest conditions experienced by any animal. The blood vessels in their feet function as heat exchangers. Warm blood pumping into the feet loses heat to the cold blood flowing back to the heart—so the feet stay cold and never get warm enough to melt the ice.

Chick sits on father's feet to stay off cold ice

BEST FOOT FORWARD

This mountain goat is climbing a steep cliff in British Columbia, Canada. Living on the steep slopes of a mountain is dangerous and only the most sure-footed animals can get around. A mountain goat's hoof is an effective piece of climbing equipment. The sharp rim of the hoof digs into the ice, helping grip the surface, while the base is covered in a spongy pad that prevents the animal from slipping. The hoof has two sections and is equivalent to an ultra-thick toenail. The two parts spread apart and grab the rough ground like a pincer, helping the animal stay standing.

ICEBERG AHEAD

The word *beluga* means "white" in Russian. That is how the beluga whale gets its name. The whale lives along the edge of the Arctic sea ice. Its white skin disguises it among the floating icebergs and helps it hide from orcas and polar bears. The beluga is hairless and keeps warm thanks to a 4-in- (10-cm-) thick layer of fatty blubber under its skin. The mammal communicates using whistles and chirps and is, therefore, nicknamed the sea canary.

Small ear reduces heat loss

In the desert

ABOUT ONE-FIFTH OF EARTH'S LAND is very dry and receives less than 10 in (250 mm) of rain in a year—barely enough to fill a bucket. These regions are deserts and range from the Sahara and other searing hot deserts around the tropics to cold deserts, such as the Gobi in central Asia. Even in hot deserts, temperatures frequently plummet at night. Few plants grow in such an inhospitable habitat. Desert animals can go for long periods without food or drink. Some travel huge distances to find scant food, while others just sit and wait, only to breed quickly during rare and sporadic rains. The Australian water-holding frog, for example, seals itself inside a bag of water to wait out a dry period.

Wedge-shaped snout slices through sand

Leg is tucked against body as lizard slithers through sand like a snake

SWIMMING IN THE SAND
A sandfish is actually a specialized skink—a type of lizard. It has a strong, cylindrical body and short legs. These help the sandfish slither—or swim—through loose sand. The creature hunts on the sand, detecting tiny vibrations made by insects scuttling around nearby. If the lizard feels threatened or gets too hot, it dives into the cool sand.

Thick fur keeps camel warm in cold, high deserts

Wing cases are fused shut, stopping body from drying out

FAT RESERVES
Water drains through sandy desert soil quickly, and so even when it rains, there are few places where plants can grow. As a result, desert browsers, such as this Bactrian camel of central Asia, have to go without eating for long periods. Amazingly, camels carry a supply of food in their humps in the form of oily fats. This allows them to go without water for 10 days and survive on the leaves of the toughest desert shrubs.

Bactrian camel has two humps

DRINKING THE FOG
The huge sand dunes of Africa's Namib Desert rise above the coast of the Atlantic Ocean. While rainfall is rare, dense banks of fog often roll in from the sea, engulfing the dunes. Fog-basking beetles sitting at the top of these sand dunes literally drink in the mist. Each beetle does a handstand, pushing its abdomen off the ground. The tiny droplets that make up the fog condense on the beetle's body and drip down tiny grooves, making their way to the beetle's mouth.

FOLLOWING THE RAIN

The Arabian oryx, a type of antelope, can go for weeks without drinking, getting all the water it needs from the plants it feeds on. Desert plants sprout soon after rain, but don't survive for long. An oryx can smell rain from many miles away and travels toward fresh plants that have grown in the wake of the rain. When not on the move, the antelope digs a cool pit in the sand under a tree and rests in the shade.

SURVIVING THE HEAT

Frogs need to stay moist in the desert heat. The Australian water-holding frog keeps damp in an amazing way. The desert pools where it breeds are very short-lived. When they dry out, the frog digs deep into the ground and cocoons itself in a bag of mucous that surrounds its skin. The cocoon hardens and forms a water-tight barrier, locking in plenty of water in and around the frog's body. The amphibian stays underground until it rains again.

KEEPING COOL

Large mammals can get very hot under the Sun. Their body temperature can rise above 106°F (41°C) to levels that would kill many mammals. Such temperatures can damage the brain of desert mammals, but a gazelle remains unaffected by this heat. It has a cooling system that cools the blood entering its brain. So even as its body heats up, its brain stays cool. This allows a gazelle being chased by a predator to keep on running, while its pursuer must stop to keep from overheating.

A gazelle's brain cooling system

Some warm blood reaches brain directly

Network of blood vessels is cooled by air in damp nostrils

Cooled blood travels back to rest of body

Sinus (chamber) is filled with cooled blood

Warm blood going to brain passes through cool sinus

Water in fog condenses on beetle's cold body

SUN SPIDERS

Deserts are home to sun spiders, some of the fiercest predators in the animal kingdom. A sun spider is about 6 in (15 cm) long and has large pincerlike mouthparts that make up one-quarter of its body. It uses its pincers to slice beetles and other insect prey. They are big enough to tackle even desert mice and snakes. Sun spiders are not true spiders, but close relatives.

Sun spider with prey

FILL THE TANK

Sandgrouse live in the dry parts of Europe, Africa, and Asia. They are seed eaters and flock into deserts when flowering plants produce seeds after a rainy period. These birds need a lot of water to digest the seeds, and they fly great distances to find watering holes. In the breeding season, the adults soak their belly feathers in water, then airlift the drinks to their chicks.

Open grassland

Pronghorn, a hoofed grassland mammal of North America

GRASSLANDS GROW IN AREAS that are too dry for forests to flourish, but not dry enough for deserts to form. There is too little rain for trees to grow but enough for fast-growing plants such as grass. The resulting oceans of grass are full of plant food for the animals that live in this habitat. There are no specific food sources to defend in territories, unlike in other habitats. Therefore, plant-eating animals, such as bulky bulls, compete over other things, such as the chance to mate. Grasslands offer a spectacular stage for watching the many struggles of animal life played out in the open.

NEED FOR SPEED
There are no places to hide on grasslands, so when danger appears, hoofed animals, such as antelopes and pronghorns, run fast. The pronghorn is capable of reaching speeds of nearly 60 mph (100 kph)—second only to the cheetah. Hoofed animals stand on their tiptoes. The bones of their feet are long, and this helps lengthen their legs and increases their stride due to the shape of their legs. It also concentrates their bulky, heavy muscles at the top of the leg, so their light, sinewy legs swing quickly and easily.

SNAKE IN THE GRASS
This reptile is not a snake, but a lizard that can slither along without legs. It lives in the grasslands of Europe and Asia, where it hunts for slugs. People named it the glass lizard because when they picked it up by the tail, the reptile appeared to break in two, like a piece of brittle glass. This mechanism helps the lizard escape easily when attacked by predators (see p.45).

TERMITES
The most important grazers (grass eaters) in some grasslands are not large hoofed mammals, but tiny insects—termites. Like an ant nest, a termite colony has a queen, but unlike an ant nest, it also has a king. Workers help this breeding pair by moving the eggs that the queen lays to the nurseries. Millions of grassland termites live in tall mounds, made of mud reinforced with dried grass. The mounds have natural cooling systems to eliminate the heat produced by the bodies of the termites.

Worker termite

Ventilation shaft

Chimney lets out rising hot air

Fungal garden grows on heaps of grass cuttings and provides food for nymphs

Nursery chamber houses nymphs (young termites)

Underground "cellar" remains cool as it draws in cool air from outside mound

Royal chamber is where queen lays eggs

NIGHT HUNTER
Grassland predators spend most of the day lazing in the shade. It is hard to keep from getting spotted by prey during daylight, so many predators wait until dark. The serval, an African cat that is about twice as big as a house cat, uses its large ears to listen for rodents rustling around in the grass. Its ears are so sensitive that it can target its pounces by sound alone.

FOLLOW THE HERD
Large herbivores, such as these wildebeest, have no reason to spread out to find food—it is all around them. Instead, they gather in herds, since it is safer for them to stay together. Every herd member looks out for danger, and when one reacts to a threat, the others follow suit. Predators usually pick off the weaker animals on the edges of a herd. Grazers form the biggest herds on the grassy plains, while browsers (herbivores that eat leaves from bushes and trees) stay in smaller groups.

SILENT STALKER

Eagles and other raptors (birds of prey) swoop over grasslands, looking to snatch anything—from a snake to a newborn antelope. However, the secretary bird hunts differently. It catches prey on foot by stalking slowly through short grass on its stiltlike legs. It watches the ground intently and when a lizard, locust, or other small animal comes out from a hiding place, this gangly bird traps its prey with its foot. It kills its victim with a rip from its hooked beak.

NESTING ON THE GROUND

While tropical grasslands, such as the African savanna, are dotted with trees, cooler grasslands, such as the American prairies, have almost no trees at all. The American burrowing owl, therefore, nests underground. It usually does not dig a den itself but sets up home in a hole vacated by another burrowing animal, such as a prairie dog. The burrow provides the owl with a shelter from predators that cannot follow the bird into the hole.

Among the trees

MORE ANIMALS ARE FOUND in forests than in any other habitat on Earth. A single tropical rainforest tree can house more than a thousand species. Rainforests are so called because they receive more than 8 ft (2.5 m) of rainfall every year, and most of them grow in the hot, damp tropics. Forests range from these hot jungles to cold conifer woodlands in the far north. In all cases, the tall trees provide hundreds of different habitats for animals. As a result, forests are home to both noisy howler monkeys that bellow from the treetops and sloths that live a very quiet life in the trees.

Cuvier's toucan

FRUITS AND NUTS
This toucan is a frugivore (fruit eater) like many forest animals. Frugivores live only in tropical forests, where constant warm temperatures allow year-round fruiting. The toucan eats the nutritious fruits and nuts produced by trees and other plants. The bird's colorful bill is long enough to reach fruits dangling from flimsy branches. The bill's jagged edge is strong enough to crack open nuts. The bill is also lightweight and does not hinder the bird's flight.

TARGET IN SIGHT
There are plenty of places to hide in a forest, and a hunter such as this vine snake has only one chance to catch a prey before it's gone. The snake has a groove that runs from each eye to the tip of its snout and works like a gun sight. The snake lines up the grooves to zero in on mice and small birds and rarely misses its targets.

Groove helps target prey accurately

HIDDEN AWAY
The jaguar is the biggest jungle cat in America. Out in the open, it is hard to see how the cat's distinctive pattern of blotchy rosettes (roselike markings) would help the predator sneak up on deer and other prey. However, in the dappled light of the forest, where the gloom is only broken by shafts of light breaking through the thick canopy of leaves, the cat's spotty fur makes for perfect camouflage, helping the cat hide.

FORAGING ON THE FLOOR
The bright colors of this giant millipede warn other animals that it may secrete nasty chemicals if attacked. Most of the time, it remains hidden away among leaf litter—the thick layer of dead leaves that covers the floor of a forest. The millipede grazes on dead plant material on the forest floor, which is also the hunting ground for predatory centipedes and blind snakes that are no larger than a worm.

Vertical pupil helps track moving insects

UP THE TREE

Tropical rainforests are very damp places, and moisture-loving frogs can easily survive high up on the branches of trees. Tree frogs use their long legs for crawling along branches. Their toes have cup-shaped suckers, which grip flat surfaces, such as large leaves. This red-eyed tree frog keeps its eyes shut tight when hiding. If threatened by a predator, the frog stares squarely at it and flashes its blue and yellow body colors. The bulging eyes and bright coloration startle the predator, scaring it away.

Tail's grip is strong enough to support weight of monkey's body

Foot is bright orange, which startles predators

Foot sole has loose skin that helps grip rough bark

GETTING NOTICED

Sometimes animals need to get noticed to attract mates. When resting with its wings folded, the blue morpho butterfly may look drab among the leaves. However, when it flies, the top of the wings are revealed, showing off a shimmering blue that stands out among the green leaves. The blue color is caused by the way light is reflected by filaments covering the butterfly's wings.

Emergent tree
125 ft (38 m)

Canopy
92 ft (28 m)

HANGING OUT

Monkeys are the fastest animals to move through the trees but when living so high up, even one foot out of place could be fatal. The new world monkeys living in South America get a helping hand from their prehensile tail, which is flexible enough to wrap around and strongly grip a branch. The tail has a hairless pad at its tip that also helps in gripping. A member of the group, this woolly monkey can hang from its tail alone as it reaches for the tastiest leaves.

THE RIGHT FIT

Jungle mammals tend to be smaller than those living in open habitats. Some scientists have suggested that the African forest elephant is a species distinct from the larger elephants living on grasslands. Being smaller helps this elephant when pushing through thick foliage. Jungle birds, on the other hand, appear to have longer bills, or beaks, than their relatives living in cooler places. The birds might use a large beak as a radiator to give out heat, so their bodies do not get dangerously hot as they fly through the steamy forest.

Understory
56 ft (17 m)

Undergrowth
16 ft (5 m)

Forest floor

MANY LEVELS

Tropical rainforests have layers that function as habitats for different groups of animals. At the top are occasional giant trees called emergents. They and the canopy trees are out in the sunshine, but they block out the light, making the forest floor a gloomy place. The canopy forms a continuous layer that is home to most rainforest animals, such as sloths. Different animals feed at different times. At night, a community of nocturnal animals emerges to feed, while the diurnal (active during day) ones hide out till dawn.

Taking to the air

I**N THE HISTORY OF LIFE** on Earth, four distinct groups of animal—insects, pterosaurs (flying reptiles), birds, and bats—evolved adaptations that enabled flight. Today, each flying animal combines a light body weight with high muscle power. It is lifted off the ground by wings. As the wings cut through the air, they create a lift force that opposes gravity and raises or holds the animal in the air. Wings developed from appendages used earlier for functions other than flight, such as gliding or balancing, camouflaging, or attracting mates. Flight evolved independently in every group of flying animal, helping unlock many new habitats.

Long fifth finger supports the wing of skin

Pterodactylus

FLYING REPTILES
The first vertebrates known to fly were the pterosaurs. These reptiles were closely related to the dinosaurs and became extinct at the same time as them—around 65 million years ago. One of the first pterosaur species to be discovered was named *Pterodactylus*, meaning "wing finger." This was because its fossils showed that much of its wing was formed by a single long finger bone with skin stretched behind it.

Small thumb has a claw that is used for gripping when bat is at rest

Primary flight feather

HANDY WINGS
Bats, which appeared around 50 million years ago, were the last group of animals to take to the air. They are the only mammals that can fly and form the mammalian order Chiroptera. Chiroptera means "hand wing" and refers to the way a bat's skin wing stretches between its finger bones. Although bats can see, many rely mostly on a system called echolocation to find their way. Bats emit high-pitched chirps that echo from objects around them. Based on the echoes, these mammals then work out the distances to the objects, forming a sound picture of their surroundings.

Wing membrane flexes over thin finger bones

Secondary flight feather

Wing is made of thin membrane running between stiff veins

Wing twists to side as it moves up, cutting through the air, but flattens before flapping down, pushing against the air

Wings are powered by muscles attached at their bases

FOUR WINGS FIRST
Insects were the first animals to fly. No other invertebrate group has taken to the air since. It is believed that the first flying insects, which appeared around 350 million years ago, had four wings and looked somewhat like today's dragonflies. Insect wings are not modified legs like the wings of birds and bats. Some biologists have suggested that insect wings may have evolved from the gills used by aquatic larvae.

Back wing moves in opposite direction from front wings in slow flight in order to reduce speed while continuing to provide the lifting force for flight

STAYING PUT

Hummingbirds survive on a diet of nectar. They do not land to feed but use their long feathery tongues to lap nectar from delicate flowers while hovering in midair. The birds beat their wings at a staggering 20 times a second to hover, making the wings look like a buzzing blur. Hummingbirds achieve this speed with the help of very flexible triangular wings. Such wings are, however, not well suited for flying long distances.

MASTERS OF THE AIR

Birds are the most varied and widespread flying animals. Different birds have different wing shapes, which enable many kinds of flying style. For example, this heron has broad wings that help in gliding slowly, while a swift has long, pointed wings that help it swoop at high speed. Wing flaps are powered by strong flight muscles that make up a bird's plump breast. These muscles comprise a third of a bird's body weight. Birds have thin, hollow bones that reduce their total weight. A lightweight body and an aerodynamic shape allow birds to fly efficiently.

Toe is very long and supports large "parachute" area

FALLING NOT FLYING

The Wallace's flying frog lives high in the trees of Southeast Asia's jungles. It leaps into the air to escape predators and to reach mates in pools on the forest floor. Once in the air, the frog spreads its large webbed feet, which break the fall like a parachute. This is not the same as flying, since the frog cannot create a lift force to push itself upward. It can only fall in a safe, controlled manner.

Neck vertebra (neck bone)

Humerus (upper arm bone)

Finger bone

Pollex (thumb bone)

Radius (a lower arm bone)

Backbone

Metacarpal (fused hand bone)

Ulna (a lower arm bone)

Hip bone

Skeleton of gray heron

Tail feather

Colored X-ray of flying fish

Tibia (shin bone)

Ankle

FINS IN A FLAP

The wings of a flying fish are stiffened fins that catch the updrafts of air pushed up by waves rolling across the surface of the ocean. The fish leaps into the air to escape attacks from predators, such as tuna. A flying fish takes off by surging along the surface, swishing its tail dozens of times a second, until it glides into the air. If a fish catches a strong gust, it can rise several yards above the water—high enough even to land on the deck of a ship.

Toe bone

Animal homes

SOME ANIMALS ARE ALWAYS on the move, searching for food and mates. Others live in one area, defending their territory from other members of their species. Still others set up temporary homes to hibernate or raise their young. A bird's nest is perhaps the best known example of an animal's home. Gorillas also build a nest of folded branches and leaves to sleep in. They seldom use the same one twice, preferring a fresh bed every night. The cave swiftlets of Southeast Asia build a home that seems far less comfortable. These birds lay their eggs in a nest made from congealed spit.

STITCHED HOMES
The masked weaver bird knits grass together to build its nest. The result is a woven ball hanging from a tree—but it is more than just a place to brood eggs. Only the male weavers build nests. Different male weavers often build their nests in a group on the same tree. When the nests are ready, female weavers inspect them. If a female likes a nest, she pairs with its builder, since she considers him to be a strong bird and a mate worthy of raising chicks with.

HOUSE OF LEAVES
Weaver ants live in trees and they make their nests out of the material available nearby—leaves. Teams of worker ants line up to haul the edges of leaves together forming a green boxlike nest. The larvae produce sticky silk that helps the adults bind the leaves together—the adults hold the larvae like tubes of glue. If the leaves are too far for an ant to reach, the workers form a chain of bodies across the gap.

Silk produced by ant larvae glues together edges of leaves

1 BEST LOCATION
The male first chooses a small branch to hang the nest from. He prefers to locate nests near the tops of trees, out of reach of tree-climbing predators, such as snakes, and often near a source of water, which will provide a steady supply of insects to feed his chicks.

DIVING BELL
The web made by a water spider is different from those created by other spiders. Instead of being a sticky fly trap like the webs found on land, the web of a water spider holds the spider's air supply during hunting dives. The spider retreats to its bubble home to digest food. Its web works like a gill, releasing waste carbon dioxide and taking in oxygen from the water. Every so often the spider refills the web with fresh air at the surface of the pond.

Case made from plant stems and pebbles

Front end enlarges as larva grows inside

A MOBILE HOME
Caddisfly larvae live in freshwater streams. Some species weave a silk tube to live in, which acts as a net to catch specks of food. Other caddisflies build more substantial homes by using their silk to glue bits of the riverbed into an armored case. This hollow case is open at both ends, and the insect ripples its body to draw water through the case. This keeps the animal supplied with oxygen and food.

Fresh, flexible stalks are easier to weave in

Size of ball-shaped nest depends on how far bird can reach

HANGING HOMES
With bodies that are adapted for flight, bats are not well suited to life on the ground. They roost in high places, crawling into crevices and clinging to large leaves. This horseshoe bat cannot even crawl, so it hangs from the roof of a cave by its back legs. Like those of other bats, its toes have a locking mechanism. The toes have a tighter grip when the foot muscles are relaxed. Therefore, the bat will not fall, even when it is asleep.

Entrance is at bottom of nest

2 IN THE LOOP
The nest starts out as a single loop of woven grasses and twigs. The bird adds more loops to build up the spherical shape of the nest. It uses its beak to weave the tips of the grass through the structure.

3 MAKE OR BREAK
If a female likes the nest, she will line its insides with more grass and some feathers. If the nest is not deemed attractive by any female, the male weaver will break it apart and build a fresh one.

MARKING TERRITORY
This otter is marking its territory, leaving its smelly droppings as scent marks—a sign that this otter controls this area. The otter finds its food within its territory and ensures that others stay away. When an otter smells the scent of another otter, it knows it is intruding into another's territory. Other animals use sounds to advertise their claims on a territory, such as the roar of a lion or bellow of a moose.

Lodge is a mound of logs and stones, sealed with mud

Sleeping chamber is above water surface

BUSY BEAVERS
A beaver's lodge is one of the greatest feats of engineering in the animal kingdom. Beavers are hefty rodents that fell small trees with their large gnawing teeth. They use the timbers to build dams on rivers, creating still-water ponds. The pond is stocked with leafy branches for the beavers to eat, and the den, or lodge, is often built in a way that it is surrounded by water so that the beavers stay safe from predators.

Dam is frequently rebuilt to maintain water level

Entrance is underwater

Migrations

A MIGRATION IS A JOURNEY that an animal undertakes, usually along a set route. It is, however, not just an aimless search for food or the same as patrolling territory. A migration has definite start and end points—sometimes thousands of miles apart—and the animal always makes a return journey, or at least its descendants do. Animals migrate in response to changes in the seasons, which make it hard for them to survive where they live. Animals of the same species often migrate together, timing their departure on a seasonal signal—such as a fall in temperature or change in the length of day. The sight of thousands of creatures on the move makes migration one of nature's great spectacles.

Birds take turns to lead flock

BIRTHING SITE
Humpback whales eat fish and krill in great gulps (see p.44). They spend the summer in the rich feeding grounds of polar seas. However, this water is too cold for newborn calves. They are born without the thick blubber that keeps the adults warm. Therefore, in winter, these whales migrate to warmer seas near the equator and give birth in quiet bays. The calves then follow their mothers, learning the route back to the feeding grounds.

Head contains a mineral called magnetite, possibly helping the bird navigate by sensing Earth's magnetic field

FOLLOWING THE STREAM
The life cycle of each of these colorful sockeye salmon is played out over one long migration. The fish start out in the headwaters of a river. As they grow, they head downstream, finally reaching the sea, where they mature over several years. The adult salmon travel all the way upriver to their birthplace to spawn (lay eggs)—turning red as they do so. The fish always head up the river in which they were born, finding it by the unique smell of its water.

Antennae are rubbed to make rasping noises that frighten attackers

WALKING THE OCEAN
These spiny lobsters form a line as they march across the sandy sea bed of the Caribbean during their fall migration to warmer waters. The lobsters also head for deeper waters, perhaps to escape the storms that disrupt their shallow summer territory. They stay within an antenna's reach of each other for protection—stragglers could easily be eaten by a predator, such as a shark or an octopus.

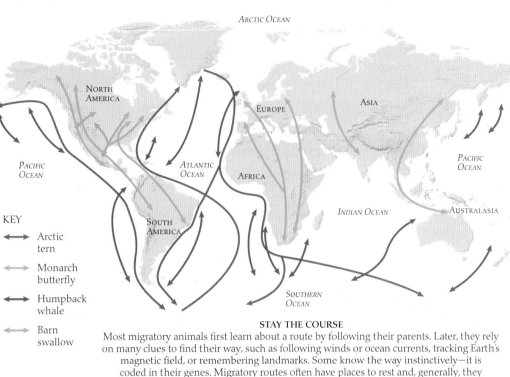

ARCTIC OCEAN

NORTH
AMERICA

EUROPE

ASIA

PACIFIC
OCEAN

ATLANTIC
OCEAN

AFRICA

PACIFIC
OCEAN

KEY

↔ Arctic
tern

↔ Monarch
butterfly

↔ Humpback
whale

↔ Barn
swallow

SOUTH
AMERICA

INDIAN OCEAN

AUSTRALASIA

SOUTHERN
OCEAN

STAY THE COURSE

Most migratory animals first learn about a route by following their parents. Later, they rely on many clues to find their way, such as following winds or ocean currents, tracking Earth's magnetic field, or remembering landmarks. Some know the way instinctively—it is coded in their genes. Migratory routes often have places to rest and, generally, they avoid difficult obstacles. Arctic terns have the longest route of all—they fly between the Arctic and Antarctic every year. In the Atlantic, the birds always fly north along an S-shaped route that takes advantage of the prevailing winds.

MOUNTAIN MEETING

The monarch butterfly is one of the few insects to migrate. These insects move south across North America each fall—around 2,800 miles (4,500 km)—and crowd into some mountain forests in Mexico and California. Millions of butterflies sit out the winter in the trees, safely above the frosty ground, before heading north again in spring. The females lay eggs on their way back and then die. New generations continue the return journey through the summer.

NORTH BOUND

These snow geese are flying north from the warmth of New Mexico. Their destination is the Arctic tundra, a treeless land that is frozen for most of the year. The geese time their arrival with the summer thaw, when countless insects swarm around boggy pools in the tundra. The geese nest in the melting landscape, feeding the bugs to their chicks. The young birds have just enough time to learn to fly before it is time to head south for the winter.

Staying alive

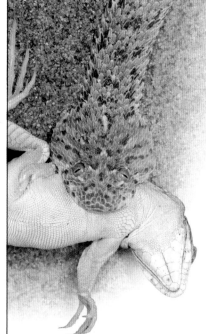

IN THE WILD, ANIMALS STRUGGLE constantly to survive. Predators must kill prey for food, while prey must always be ready to fend off a predator's attack. Both predator and prey are in a race to stay a step ahead of each other. An interesting example is a race for survival between a mouse and a venomous snake, in which each animal adapts constantly in the presence of an evolving foe. If the mouse becomes resistant to the snake's venom, the snake evolves in ways that make it more toxic. Biologists call this the Red Queen Effect, named after the character from the book *Through the Looking Glass* who is always running but appears to stay in the same place because everything around her is also moving. This mirrors how predator and prey evolve constantly, but neither gains an advantage over the other.

HIDDEN TRICKSTER
The Peringuey's adder lives in the deserts of southwest Africa. Its lizard prey move cautiously across the sand, looking for threats. However, this snake is not easy to spot—its rough scales match the sand and so it can lie hidden, waiting to ambush prey, such as this gecko. The snake lures the lizard within biting distance by wiggling the dark tip of its tail above the sand. The adder then kills its prey with its venom—poisonous saliva that paralyzes the lizard in seconds.

Dry outer strand is held by spider

TRAPS OF SILK
The oger-faced spider eats insects that walk on the ground. These insects pick up the vibrations of ground-based predators and scuttle clear of shadows that might indicate an approaching bird. But this long-legged spider avoids detection by hanging motionless just above the ground, flexing a sticky net in its four front legs. The spider's huge eyes scan the ground until an insect walks under the net, which is then dropped with lightning speed. As the insect struggles, it becomes totally tangled and is then killed with a bite from the spider.

Whale dives to create bubble net

Ball of fish driven to surface

Waiting whale

Whale keeps blowing bubbles

Eye spot looks like iris and pupil

Waiting whale's calls scare fish into a tight shoal

Spiral path followed by whale toward surface

Bubble net begins to form

BUBBLE NETS
Humpback whales can fit hundreds of fish into every mouthful, and eating a few at a time would take far too long to fill their stomachs. So the whales band together to feed more efficiently by herding fish into tight shoals, perfect for eating in great gulps. The whales swim in a spiral, blowing a wall of bubbles around the fish, making them crowd together. Several whales can net shoals more than 65-ft (20-m) wide. When the fish are near the surface, the whales surge up from below with their mouths open, eating their fill.

MIMICS
This owl butterfly would ideally make an easy meal for a tree frog in its rainforest home. But the hungry frog stays away from it because when the butterfly opens its wings, two dark spots are exposed on them because of the movement. This fools the frog into believing that it is looking into the eyes of an owl or another large animal. The frog gets scared and leaves the butterfly alone.

DIVING DOWN
A kingfisher has evolved eyes that allow it to spot fish before entering the water, from a high perch on a tree well out of sight of its prey. Water refracts, or bends, light so the bird has to adjust its eyes when targeting underwater prey. Each of the bird's eyes has two focus centers—the eyes of most animals have just one. The kingfisher uses the first to spot the fish from the perch and switches to the other once it dives in. The cells in a kingfisher's eyes have a drop of pigmented oil that probably filters out the glare from water, which may otherwise make it difficult for the bird to spot prey in water.

SPRAYING ACID
Of all the thousands of ants in a colony, only the queen ant actually produces young, and so it is common for worker ants to sacrifice their lives to protect her, fighting attackers to death. To ward off predators, wood ants employ a chemical weapon. They squirt a burning chemical called formic acid from their abdomens. This is the same acid that causes the sharp burning pain after a bee sting.

*Transparent eyelid
slides across to
protect eye in water*

Tail regenerating slowly

LOST TAIL
This tree skink was attacked by a predator. It survived, but lost its tail. The tree skink has a quick-release bone at the base of its tail, which snaps off so if grabbed by the tail, the lizard can escape. The predator is left with the detached tail that continues to wriggle. The skink grows a new tail but this will not detach in the next attack, since the tail cannot regenerate more than once.

Living together

Animals frequently rely on another animal species for their survival. Such a link is called symbiosis, which means "together living" in Ancient Greek. The partners don't always live close together, but they often depend on each other for mutual benefit. Each relationship between two species is unique and is based on the ways the animals live. There are three kinds of symbiosis, and perhaps the most common is parasitism, in which only one species benefits from the relationship, while the other—known as the host—is weakened by it. Parasites include tapeworms living in the gut and blood-sucking insects. Mutualism is a relationship in which both species benefit, while commensalism is halfway between the two—one animal benefits, while the other is completely unaffected.

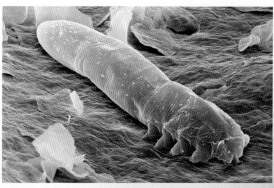

TINY PASSENGER
About 50 percent of people live in symbiosis with this microscopic eyelash mite. This mite sets up home in the follicle (a small sac or cavity from which a hair grows) of the human eyelash, eating oily flakes of skin. This mite is an ectoparasite—one that lives on the outside of its host's body. Few people suffer problems from hosting these mites.

Plaintive cuckoo chick

CUCKOO IN THE NEST
The larger bird in this picture is a chick. It is being fed by a male sunbird, but this bird is not the chick's father. The chick is a cuckoo, and its mother laid the egg in the sunbird's nest without being spotted. The cuckoo is a brood parasite—an animal that tricks another into raising its young. Although the cuckoo's egg is larger, it looks a lot like a sunbird egg, so the sunbird fails to recognize that the egg is not its own. Once the cuckoo chick hatches, it ejects any sunbird chicks or unhatched sunbird eggs from the nest, so that it alone can eat the food brought to the nest by the sunbird parent.

Wingless aphid sucks sap constantly

APHID FARMS
Aphids are insects that drink the sap running through plant stems. Because of this purely liquid diet, the little aphids produce a lot of sugary urine, which is known as honeydew. For many types of ant, honeydew is a good source of food. Some will even stand guard over a herd of aphids, keeping away predators while the aphids feed. In return for providing this protection, the ants milk the aphids, stroking them until they produce sweet droplets of honeydew. This relationship is an example of mutualism.

Male
mariqua
sunbird

PECKING TO ORDER

The oxpecker is a relative of the starling. It lives among the large herds of grazing mammals that roam across the grasslands of Africa. The bird is often seen riding larger animals, such as this zebra, balancing during bumpy rides on its stiff tail. It slides its flat beak between the hairs of the host to pluck ticks and lice from its host's skin. The zebra gets a cleaning service, while the bird is rewarded with a rich diet of bloodsucking parasites. The oxpecker may also act as a parasite, feeding on blood from an open wound on the body of the zebra.

Big eye gives watchman goby its name

TEAMING UP

The watchman goby and the pistol shrimp form a partnership on the sandy seabed. The goby shares the burrow that the shrimp digs. The fish acts as the short-sighted shrimp's lookout. The shrimp frequently checks if its partner is in place with its long antennae. If danger approaches, the goby flicks the shrimp with its tail, and the duo dash into the burrow.

Ridged sucker is formed from a flattened dorsal fin

Shrimp works to keep the burrow clean

Hyena growls while standing over its food in a defensive posture

Remora

GOING WITH THE FLOW

Commensalism is rare compared to the other forms of symbiosis. An example of a commensal is the remora. This slender fish sticks itself to large sharks, rays, and whales, using a sucker on the top of its head. The fish eats its host's droppings or the leftovers from the host's meals. The larger animal gains nothing from carrying the hitchhiker, and the remora's streamlined shape means that it does not slow down its transporter either.

Black-backed jackal is fully alert and ready to escape, should the hyena attack

THIEVING CARNIVORES

Spotted hyenas sometimes hunt for prey, but they usually scavenge, feasting on the carcasses of dead animals. Often a gang of hyenas will steal food from a hunter, such as a big cat, chasing it away from its kill. This thieving behavior is called kleptoparasitism. However, the hyena's meal is not safe either. Another kleptoparasite, the black-backed jackal, may be looking to snatch a bite.

Living in groups

Humans are not the only animals that live in societies. While many animals fend for themselves and prefer to live alone, some live in groups. There are advantages and disadvantages to being a social animal. The biggest difficulty is that group members have to share many things. They must eat what they can from the same supply of food, and, in many cases, all the adult males may have to compete for the same females in the group. Despite these problems, the members of a group stick together. Often it is because they cannot survive without teaming up. In all cases, animal societies function as a delicate balance where the gains outweigh the losses.

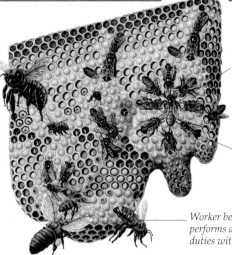

Queen bee lays eggs in honeycomb of cells

Young worker bee tends to the eggs of the queen bee

Worker bee is a female that performs a wide variety of duties within the nest

SOCIAL BEES
Honeybees are truly social, or eusocial, and have an advanced level of social organization that is also seen in ants, termites, some wasps, and even rodents. A single female—the queen bee—produces the offspring. More than 600 new larvae hatch from eggs every day. The rest of the society is made up of her daughters, who work to raise their younger sisters—and occasionally brothers, or drones, who fly off to mate with young queens. The worker bees never produce young of their own. They collect nectar from flowers to make honey, which they use along with pollen to feed themselves and the army of young.

PAIRING UP
The smallest animal group is a breeding pair. Lovebirds—small species of parrot—get their name from the way a male and a female pair up for life. Even if the two birds spend long periods apart, when the breeding season comes around, they meet up and raise chicks together. This single-mate system is called monogamy. Monogamous pairs work together to protect the young and maximize their chances of survival. Many bird species are monogamous, but monogamy is quite rare in other animals. Monogamous mammals include the beaver.

Fisher's lovebirds

SUPERPODS AT SEA
Dolphins and whales live in family groups called pods. A typical pod contains about 15 animals and is made up of females, their calves, and a tight-knit gang of males that have grown up in various other pods. When several pods converge at one place to feed, a superpod forms. In some species, dolphins from one pod mingle with strangers from other pods and may opt to join a new group for a while.

RANK AND FILE

Hamadryas baboons of East Africa and Arabia live in a highly ordered society. A troop of around 400 monkeys sleeps together on the cliffs of their arid habitat—a defense tactic against nocturnal predators. Every monkey has a rank in the group, and the young males are always ready to take over from an older, weakening male. Big adult males rule over a harem of females, and several harems band together as a clan—one of many per troop. Males frequently fight over females, and if any monkey steps out of line, it is punished with a bite.

Dominant male has tufts of gray fur

Baby travels with its mother

Young male is not allowed to mate with females

Female may be stolen by male from another harem

HUNTING IN A TEAM

The wolf is one of the few animals that can kill prey that is bigger than it is. It does this by working in a team, or pack. Wolves can follow prey for hours on end without getting tired, so the pack chases prey, such as an injured deer, taking turns biting their victim until it crashes to the ground exhausted. A pack of 12 wolves can kill a 1,100-lb (500-kg) moose. A wolf hunting alone might be able to bag only a 4.5-lb (2-kg) rabbit.

Wolves howl to warn other packs in the area to stay away

POPULATION EXPLOSION

Locust swarms are some of the largest groups of animals, containing billions of insects. These large grasshoppers normally live on their own, but crowd together in search of food. Increased levels of body contact cause the insects to produce a different kind of young that hop away. The wingless hoppers gather into large groups and transform into long-winged adults that fly off as a swarm. They are strong enough to fly for 20 hours at a time. When the swarm lands, the locusts eat entire fields of crops.

ONE OF THE CROWD

Seabirds, such as these gannets, crowd together on cliffs to raise their chicks. They nest together in huge colonies, called rookeries, on rocky islets and cliffs so inaccessible that egg eaters, such as rats, cannot reach them. The parents take turns diving for food out at sea, bringing some back for the chicks. To ensure that the returning gannet has landed at the correct nest, mates greet each other by tapping beaks—to confirm that it is the right bird.

The human animal

It is sometimes easy to ignore the fact that human beings are animals. The scientific name for the human species is *Homo sapiens* and it belongs to a group of mammals called the primates. The animals most closely related to humans are chimpanzees. These two species share at least 98 percent of their DNA (see p.14). However, the remaining bit of DNA is enough to make the two primates very different. Modern humans evolved around 150,000 years ago, several million years after chimpanzees first appeared. In the time since then—mostly in the last 10,000 years—humans have had a greater impact on life on Earth than any other species in the history of the planet.

Rounded skull is positioned on top of neck

Barrel-shaped rib cage allows arms to swing, helping balance body when human walks on two legs

Spine (backbone) forms S-shaped curve and helps absorb shocks while walking

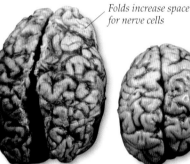

Folds increase space for nerve cells

A COMPLEX BRAIN
Humans have the largest brain in the animal kingdom, when compared to their body size. For example, it is significantly larger than the brain of a gorilla—a close relative that is larger and heavier than a human. The human brain is incredibly complex. It has 120 billion nerve cells that communicate via a staggering million billion connections. That is 5,000 times the number of stars in our galaxy!

Human brain   Gorilla brain

USING MEDICINE
Scientific research has shown that some mammals, such as dogs and non-human primates, such as chimpanzees, eat certain plants when they feel sick. This is called self-medication—something that humans also do, but in unique ways. Humans use medicines—that often contain products from plants—to battle illnesses. Many cultures have traditionally used meadowsweet and willow for making painkilling drinks. These plants contain aspirin, a painkiller used by millions of people.

Painkilling tablets

Meadowsweet

Wide pelvis, cradling and supporting the soft organs above

Thigh bones are angled inward toward knees and keep upper body over the hips for balance while walking

ON TWO LEGS
These skeletons highlight some of the anatomical differences between humans and one of their closest relatives, the gorilla. These differences are a result of the different ways in which these animals walk. Most primates, such as gorillas, move short distances on their hind legs but are normally quadripedal—they walk on all fours. Humans are bipedal mammals, who walk upright on two feet. There are many theories about why humans became bipedal. It may have helped them see farther than quadripedal primates or freed up their hands to collect berries.

Farmer working in rice field

GROWING FOOD
For most of human history, humans have been hunters and gatherers. Early humans ate whatever they could find, killing animals occasionally, but surviving mainly on seeds, roots, and fruits. About 10,000 years ago, humans learned to grow food plants, such as rice and wheat, by following the seasons to yield harvests. This was the birth of farming. Humans are also the only animals who cook their food before eating it.

Heel and toes of foot touch ground, helping human walk

Human skeleton

GLOBAL ANIMAL

Electric lights show up all over Earth at night, indicating human settlements clustered in different areas around the globe. Humans evolved in Africa, spreading across Europe, Asia, and Australia about 40,000 years ago and reaching the Americas around 14,000 years ago. Humans are also the only vertebrates to stay in the frozen continent of Antarctica all through the year—there has been a permanent settlement at the South Pole since 1956.

USING TOOLS

Many animals use simple tools—chimpanzees, for instance, strip twigs to collect termites—but none of them can match the complexity of tools created by human beings. Our ancestor *Homo habilis* was a human species that used stone cutters about 2.5 million years ago. The human toolkit has grown since then, moving from wood, bone, and stone, to pottery and metal objects. This pocket knife is a versatile tool that helps cut and shred objects as well as open cans. Complex modern tools include computer chips and plastics derived from crude oil.

Cone-shaped rib cage allows flexibility of shoulder joints, helping gorilla reach above its head when climbing

LIVING TOGETHER

There are 7 billion people on Earth, and most live in crowded communities. In prehistoric times, groups of about 150 people lived together on the African grasslands, teaming up to survive. Today, most of us can remember the names and faces of about the same number of friends. When we meet friends, we exchange news using language, an efficient way of bonding big groups together. In contrast, chimpanzees in a troop stay friends by grooming each other—and while humans accept strangers, our ape cousins would attack them on sight.

Long, narrow pelvis helps walking on all fours, but does not support internal organs when ape stands

Thigh bones are parallel to each other

Gorilla skeleton

Knuckle rests on ground when walking on all fours

Big toe grasps objects, helping ape climb

Livestock

THOUSANDS OF YEARS AGO, humans began to domesticate and rear useful animals, using them for their muscle power, products, and body parts. Prehistoric humans in North America used antlers as digging sticks, while those in Africa transported water inside ostrich eggs. Sheep and goats were domesticated around 8,000 years ago—they were probably the first farm animals (livestock). Gradually, the list of livestock grew to include cattle, pigs, and chickens. Farmers paired up the animals with the most useful traits, breeding them together so that their offspring would also have these traits. As a result of this artificial breeding, modern livestock is tame and produces large quantities of useful commodities, such as milk and wool.

Horn is partly shaped by human owner as it grows

OWNER'S PRIDE
The word cattle comes from the Old French word *chatel*, meaning property. In several societies, herds of cattle are symbols of wealth and status. These zebus (humped cattle), for instance, belong to the Dinka people of Southern Sudan. Every dry season, most of the Dinka leave their homes to follow their huge herd to grassy pastures. A single cow provides manure (used as fertilizer and fuel), milk, and even blood to drink. When a zebu dies, its skin is made into leather. Zebu meat is eaten only on very special occasions.

The aurochs was the ancestor of modern domestic cattle

The Scottish Aberdeen Angus is bred for good quality meat

THEN AND NOW
The domestic cow is a descendant of a huge grazer called the aurochs. Once spread across Europe and Asia, the aurochs became extinct in 1627. Zebus (main picture) are descended from Indian aurochs and are suited to life in hot, dry places. Beef cattle, such as the Aberdeen Angus and the world's most productive dairy breeds, are related to European aurochs.

A LIVING ANCESTOR
Every domestic animal is a descendant of a wild ancestor. Many of these wild animals are extinct or have become very rare, and their domestic counterparts make up most of the population of the species. However, this is not true of the red jungle fowl. Believed to be the wild form of the chicken, the red jungle fowl is still widespread in the wild. Males display the same vibrant features of a farmyard rooster, and as in domestic flocks, the bird follows a strict social system, or pecking order.

Red jungle fowl rooster

WILD INSIDE
Despite centuries of captive breeding to shape domestic animals into tame and productive creatures, a few of them still exhibit some of their wild character. For example, sheep are descended from the mouflon—a species of small and sturdy grazers that lived in the rocky mountains of western Asia. These sure-footed creatures would dash up steep slopes to escape from less agile attackers. Sheep display a similar behavior—they run uphill when frightened.

BETTER SWEATER

For millennia, humans have used fur of other mammals to stay warm in cold climates. Long and thin woolly hairs can be spun into strands or yarn and used to weave warm clothing. Wool comes not only from sheep, but also from alpacas, camels, and goats. Garments made of perhaps the softest wool come from the fluffy hairs of angora rabbits. Their hair shafts are hollow, which makes the wool light and warm.

BUG TO DYE FOR

In the 16th century, red dyes in Europe were too expensive for all but the wealthiest families. Spanish settlers in South America were, therefore, intrigued by how the local people dyed their clothes deep red. They found that insects called cochineal bugs, which live on cacti, produced a defensive chemical that was used to make the dye. Today, the bugs are grown in large plantations, and the unusual dye has applications from dyeing food to coloring lipsticks.

SILK ROUTE

The Silk Route—an ancient trade route that ran east to west across Asia—was named after silk, the most lucrative product to be traded along it. Fine silks from China fetched huge sums in the West, where the secret of their production was unknown. Silk cloth is woven from strands produced by silkworms, which are actually moth caterpillars that live on mulberry tree leaves. Hundreds of silkworms can be seen above at a breeding base in Matou town, China. Silkworms were domesticated about 4,700 years ago. Today, they survive only in captivity.

Animal workers

The first working animals may have acted as guards. These half-tamed wolves may have lived alongside humans about 15,000 years ago. Their enhanced senses of smell and hearing enabled them to detect approaching danger. These animals barked to warn the humans before they could sense the threat themselves. Today, humans use many animals for their natural abilities. Carrier pigeons, for instance, can find their way home from almost anywhere, making them perfect for carrying secret messages for humans. Animals are also used for their great strength. Before the invention of engines, many machines, such as wheeled carts and water pumps, were powered by animals.

TO THE RESCUE
This search-and-rescue dog uses its sense of smell to find people buried in snow by avalanches. These dogs are very good at sniffing out people because the section of a dog's brain used to detect odors is 40 times bigger than the equivalent part of a human brain. Also, there are about 200 million smell receptors inside a dog's wet nose, whereas humans have just about 5 million. As a result, a dog's sense of smell is far superior to a human's.

Tracking device attached to flipper

ANIMAL SOLDIERS
This bottlenose dolphin works for the US Navy. The brain of a dolphin is larger than that of a human, but not as complex. Nevertheless, the dolphin is highly intelligent and can be trained to recognize enemy mines suspended in the water. Other navy dolphins are trained to search for injured human divers and help them to the surface. The US military also uses trained sea lions to clip tracking devices on to enemy scuba divers.

HARD WORKER
A mule's father (sire) is a donkey but its mother (dam) is a horse. Being a mix, or hybrid, of two species, mules cannot produce young of their own—they are born to work as beasts of burden. Mules have the best features of their parents. They are big and strong like a horse, but calm and sure-footed like a donkey. That makes them ideal for carrying heavy loads along treacherous mountain paths.

CATCHING FISH

The cormorant is an expert fish catcher, and Chinese fishermen have been using the bird's skills for more than a thousand years. The fisherman ties a loose snare around the base of a cormorant's long neck and sends it to dive for fish. The snare allows the bird to swallow the small fishes it catches, but the bigger ones get stuck. When the bird returns to the boat, its owner eases the fish from the bird's throat—and keeps it for himself.

Long, flexible neck helps grab fish

China statuette of Lippizan dancing horse

DANCING HORSES

Lippizan horses come from Slovenia. These horses have descended from Spanish and North African varieties and were bred to be strong and agile. While adult Lippizans are white, the foals are born much darker. Some stallions of this breed are trained to dance at the Spanish Riding School in Vienna, Austria, and the breed is best known for this.

EASY TO STUDY

Scientists use little fruit flies from the genus *Drosophila* to study the way genes work. Genes are arranged on structures called chromosomes inside cells. These insects have large chromosomes that are easy to study. Scientists change a fly's genetic structure to see how it alters the way the insect grows. After genetic alteration, this fly has grown extra wings. *Drosophila* flies breed very quickly, taking just a few days to go from an egg to an adult, and therefore, many experiments can be carried out on them.

Extra pair of wings grows due to added genes

False-color image of a fruit fly with modified genetic structure

PEST CONTROLLER

The mongoose is a small carnivore that lives in Asia and Africa. Many species are good at killing snakes, and in some countries, they are used as pest controllers, clearing dangerous snakes from houses and gardens. A mongoose can tackle even a cobra, one of the most venomous snakes. While a bite from this snake could kill a human, the agile mongoose darts clear of most strikes and is immune to the cobra's venom.

HIDDEN GUARD

This Great Pyrennees is one of a breed of large dogs used to protect flocks of sheep from attacks by wolves, lynxes, and bears, in the mountains between France and Spain. It has been bred to be a "dog in sheep's clothing"—its shaggy white fur helps it mingle with the flock without spooking the timid sheep. The sheep soon grow used to its presence, and the dog is ready to attack any intruders threatening the flock in the same way it would attack while protecting a pack of dogs.

Shaggy white fur

Sheep remain calm in dog's presence

Friends and companions

PEOPLE OFTEN MAKE ROOM in their families for animals kept as companions. The most popular pets are cats and dogs—there are several hundred million of them, many more than their counterparts surviving in the wild. People also keep other animals as pets, from deadly snakes to tiny insects. Unlike their wild-living relatives, pets never have to search for food, but relatively few of them get a chance to mate and produce young.

Border collie catches a toy in the air

MANY BREEDS
Each dog breed has certain characteristics. For example, this border collie is intelligent and can follow instructions from its master. Collies are working dogs, commonly used as sheep dogs, but they can learn tricks and play games and, therefore, make rewarding companions. The tiny chihuahua breed—the same species as a collie or wolf—could not be more different. This tiny Mexican dog is 10 times smaller than a wolf and was bred to be easy to carry, stroke, and cuddle.

THE WOLF WITHIN
All pet dogs are descended from wild wolves. Dogs and humans are both social species, which makes it easier for them to live together. Wolf packs began living alongside humans about 15,000 years ago. The wolves scavenged on waste food, and once domesticated, they may have teamed up with humans for hunts. Over the centuries, dogs have been bred into many varieties, or breeds, each with a set of specific characteristics.

ALL IN THE FAMILY
Hamsters have pouches in their cheeks that store seeds, a useful feature in these desert rodents, as they can go for many days without finding food. These pouches give the hamsters cute, rounded faces. In the 1930s, hamsters became fashionable pets. The craze began when a female hamster and her 12 offspring were taken from the wild in Syria and bred as pets. It is believed that all the world's captive golden hamsters (the most popular pet species of all hamsters) are descendants of that single female.

Skin has blue-gray patches

CREEPY PETS
Some people like to keep dangerous animals—or at least ones that look dangerous—as pets. Many people consider the tarantula to be a deadly spider. It was believed that a tarantula's bite produced dangerous frenzies. The spider was named after a fast-paced Italian dance, the *tarentella*. However, a tarantula's bite is largely harmless to humans and these spiders are kept as pets by many.

MUTANT CREATURES
Some breeds of pet are mutants that could not survive in the wild. This strange-looking sphynx cat is descended from a single Canadian cat that was born hairless in 1966. Sphynx cats suffer in cold weather without a covering of hair and would not survive outside a warm house. Other mutant pets include albino snakes that have no natural camouflage and lop-eared rabbits that cannot hear approaching danger as well as rabbits in the wild can.

WINGED COMPANIONS

Parrots are famous for the way they can copy sounds, such as the ring of a telephone or the flush of a toilet. They even repeat the words people say, which is very enjoyable for their owners. An organ called the syrinx, or voice box, in their throats allows parrots to produce a wide range of sounds. Most parrots are too large to keep in a cage, but budgerigars—little parrots from Australia—make good pets.

Parrots are good mimics because in the wild they communicate using a local set of calls, which they learn by copying older parrots.

Color of feathers is determined by selective breeding

Japanese children playing with goldfish (19th-century illustration)

FISH IN A BOWL

For thousands of years, people have kept fish—especially meaty carp—in ponds as a source of food. About 1,000 years ago—probably first in China—people began keeping carp as pets. Over the years, people created eye-catching breeds such as goldfish and koi, which are now found in aquariums across the world. Fish use bright colors to attract mates, and many vibrant species from coral reefs and tropical rivers are also popular pets today.

THE WILD SIDE

The dingo is one of Australia's most widespread animals. It was introduced to the continent about 4,000 years ago when people brought pet dogs over from Southeast Asia. These dogs escaped and became feral (reverted to a wild state). Soon, dingoes became one of the main predators in Australia. Dingoes live in loose packs but generally hunt alone for rabbits and small kangaroos.

Pests

In nature, there is no such thing as a pest, but humans label some animals "pests" when they damage crops, harm domestic animals, or spread diseases. Humans, meanwhile, have a very large impact on the environment—we turn wild land into fields and cities. While most animals lose areas of their habitat in this process, a few species benefit and thrive in artificial landscapes. For example, bedbugs evolved long before people invented beds. They sucked the blood of bats and birds roosting in caves—and then switched to feeding on the early humans who moved in later. These tiny insects can now be found wherever humans sleep, and like many pests, have spread across the world.

CITY SLACKERS
The pigeons living in cities are feral—they are descended from domestic pigeons that were once kept for food or for carrying messages. The wild relatives of pigeons are called rock doves, which roost on steep cliffs. The tall stone buildings of most cities make an equally good habitat. City pigeons feed on a constant diet of waste food and breed four or five times a year. Pigeon droppings can be found all over cities. They are not only smelly, but also cause speedy erosion of buildings.

FRUIT KILLER
Helix aspersa, a species of land snail, is native to Europe. It is better known as the garden snail because it is often seen grazing on leaves in vegetable patches and on fruit trees. In the last 150 years, this snail has spread to many other regions of the world by hitching rides on plant produce being moved by humans from one place to another. Today, the garden snail has become a pest in California's valuable orange orchards.

PEST AT HOME
Cockroaches live wherever there is rotting waste, such as leftover food. These pests originated in humid African jungles but have set up home in basements and sewers across the world. The tough insects have even turned up at a military base near the North Pole. Cockroaches are good at staying out of sight. The insects scavenge in the dark and scuttle quickly into cracks when lights are turned on. Cockroaches can carry diseases.

ACCIDENTAL PEST
In the 1930s, sugar cane crops in Australia were being ruined by beetles. Giant toads from South America were introduced to eat up these pests. These ground-dwelling toads ate the beetles when available, but often could not reach the beetles high up in the canes. The plantations were also too dry, so these cane toads left the sugar cane and the beetles and spread in their millions across eastern Australia. They eventually became a bigger nuisance—these poisonous toads caused a decline in the populations of many native predators, such as many species of monitor lizard.

DEADLY BLOODSUCKER
Mosquitoes are pests because they spread deadly diseases. Female mosquitoes drink the blood of humans and other animals—to get the nutrients they need to grow eggs. When biting an animal, the mosquitoes secrete saliva into the blood of the animal. This saliva may carry germs that can cause diseases, such as yellow fever, elephantiasis, and malaria. These diseases are all dangerous—malaria alone kills 750,000 people every year.

Only female has long mouthpart that sucks blood

MAKING A NUISANCE
Some animals are considered pests because they just make things messy. Moles are seldom seen, but the hills of soil they produce when digging fresh tunnels ruin a neat lawn. The hills appear in lines as the mole pushes out excavated soil. Moles that dig under trees produce fewer molehills because the tree roots support the burrows better than the roots of grass and so the animals don't need to push out as much soil.

Cercus is a small hair on the abdomen that detects air currents created by an attacker approaching from behind

DUMMY HUNTERS
Animals become pests when they are taken out of their natural habitats and away from predators that keep their populations from getting too large. However, pests continue to be on the lookout for threats in human settlements just like they would do in the wild. Dummies of predators, such as this lifelike model owl, are often kept perched above fields and gardens to scare away crows and seed-eating birds. Humans also use these dummies in parking lots and other places that face a problem of bird droppings.

BRINGER OF DEATH
When a pest species arrives in a new area it can cause devastation. Black rats did just that. Originally from Asia, they spread along trade routes by stowing away on ships. They reached Europe around 2,000 years ago. The fleas living on the rats carried a disease called the plague. The worst outbreak of plague—termed the Black Death—was in the 14th century, when 100 million people were killed. The last major outbreak of the plague in England was in 1665, when more than 100,000 people died. This illustration shows an infected woman lying on a road.

Protecting animals

HUMAN ACTIVITIES affect the natural environment, creating problems for wild animals. Humans continue to remove wild habitats, replacing them with farmland and settlements and using natural resources for the growing human population. These areas support only a few wild animals. Some animals, such as pests or farm animals, thrive under the changes, but most others find life much harder. They may face a shortage of food or places to raise their young, resulting in a drop in their numbers. Many wild animals have also been hunted to extinction by humans. At least 700 species have become extinct because of human activities. Some 21,000 other species—probably many more—are threatened or endangered and could die out, too.

POLLUTION
These fish have died after crude oil was spilled in the water, filling it with poisons. This is an example of pollution, which is the presence of harmful substances in the environment in unnatural amounts. A polluting substance is called a pollutant, and it is most often a chemical released into water or air from homes or factories. Pollutants can also be excessive heat or noises emitted by vehicles and machines, as well as excessive light—anything that prevents an animal from living in an area.

HUNTING THE HUNTER
A tiger is strong enough to knock a buffalo off its feet and kill it with one bite. However, even this top predator has enemies—human hunters. People hunt tigers for their skin, to sell body parts as traditional medicines, and sometimes just for sport. Despite their formidable strength, tigers are unable to protect themselves against hunting rifles. In the last 100 years alone, the number of tigers has fallen by 95 percent. Today, there are only about 4,000 left.

DAMAGED HABITATS
One of the ways in which humans endanger animals is by damaging their habitats or even wiping out the habitats completely. The ʻiʻiwi bird of Hawaii has a curved beak that helps it sip nectar from certain flowers unique to Hawaii. These flowers have become rare, replaced by new plant species introduced by humans. The ʻiʻiwi now feeds almost exclusively on flowers from the ʻōhiʻa tree, which is also becoming rare. Without this tree, the bird could become extinct.

ʻIʻiwi bird feeds on flowers of an ʻōhiʻa tree

CHANGING FAST
In the Arctic Ocean, walruses rest on ice floes (floating ice) after diving to the seabed to hunt for shellfish. The area of sea ice in the Arctic has gone down in recent years, most probably due to the way humans have altered Earth's climate. Climates and habitats are always changing—that is what drives evolution. However, natural changes are slow compared to human activities that may be changing the world too rapidly for evolution to keep up.

TRADE BANS

Animals hunted in the wild are often protected by law. A ban on the trade of ivory makes it illegal to sell this elephant tusk anywhere in the world. With this trade ban, the world's governments hoped to reduce the number of elephants poached (illegally killed) for the ivory in their tusks. Between 1979 and 1989, the population of African elephants almost halved because of poaching. The ivory was carved into valuable trinkets. Since the ban, elephant numbers have been rising.

Tag glued to seal's skin transmits location data to a satellite

STUDYING ANIMALS

Sometimes animals suddenly become rare without obvious reasons. To understand such mysteries, scientists must gather information about the environment. This harbor seal lives in an area polluted by an oil spill, which has affected its numbers. The seal has been fitted with a tag that records where the seal goes as it looks for fish to eat. This helps the experts build up a map of which areas of ocean have recovered from the spill and which are still polluted.

Walrus uses its tusks to climb on to ice floe

Children watch a penguin parade at Edinburgh Zoo, UK

LEARNING TO CARE

Protecting endangered animals is called conservation, and one of the most important jobs of a conservationist is teaching people why it is important to look after animals in the wild. In addition to being fun places to see animals up close, zoos are places where visitors can get to know about how they can help threatened animals. Without conservation programs, many animals would only survive in zoos.

Tourists view animals from safety of a van

PAYING FOR PROTECTION

Conservation activities are very expensive, but they can pay for themselves. Tourists pay high prices for safari rides, in which they can observe animals closely in the wild. Safari vehicles, such as these vans, are a common sight in East Africa's national parks. People also tour rainforests hoping to spot a tiger or take boat trips to find whales. National parks and ecotourism companies use the money from the tourists to protect the animals and their natural environments and so ensure that the tourists keep coming.

Animals in mythology

Myths and legends from around the globe often feature animals that can do amazing things—not the least of which is the ability to talk to one another. Mythical monsters, such as the snake-haired gorgons or one-eyed cyclops, may be like nothing on Earth, but some supernatural creatures can have a basis in the natural world. For example, the magic salmon eaten by Irish giant Finn McCool as a boy made him the world's wisest man—in real life, fish oils aid brain development. In a similar way, the mythical phoenix has a real-life counterpart—the Tongan megapode bird. The phoenix is a firebird that appears from the hot ashes of its burning mother, while the Tongan megapode bird incubates its eggs in the warm ash of a volcano!

SOMETHING FISHY

Mermaids are among the most familiar of mythical creatures. They are said to look like women with a fish tail instead of legs. For thousands of years, sailors returning from long, difficult voyages told stories of beautiful mermaids in the water. It is possible that the sailors—when exhausted and thirsty—mistook dugongs or manatees swimming around their ships for mermaids. Dugongs and manatees are not pretty. They are heavy, grazing sea mammals collectively known as sea cows.

Long crest formed by first few rays of dorsal fin

Scaleless skin covered in slime

SERPENT OR NOT?

The oarfish is the nearest thing nature has to a sea serpent. This slender animal can grow up to 56 ft (17 m) in length—longer than any other fish. It lives in the dark depths of the seas but occasionally appears at the surface. Rare sightings of this animal make quite a story and people like to hear incredible tales. It is these tales that have stretched a harmless oarfish into a monstrously long sea serpent capable of destroying ships with its coils.

Camera inside watertight box

SEARCHING FOR NESSIE

This underwater "Creature Camera" was used in the 1970s to look for the world's most famous cryptid, the Loch Ness Monster. A cryptid is an animal that many people report they have seen but which has not been recognized by scientists. The camera found nothing. "Nessie" is said to be an immense reptile that lurks in the deep waters of Britain's largest lake, but scientists say there is not enough food in the cold lake for such a large animal.

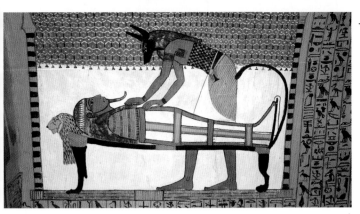

JACKAL-HEADED GOD

The ancient Egyptians preserved the bodies of dead people as mummies in order to help them on their journey to the afterlife. They believed that the dead followed the God Anubis on their way to the afterlife—this painting shows Anubis standing over the mummy of a dead craftsman. Anubis was thought to have the body of a man and the head of a jackal—this is not surprising, since jackals were common in the ancient cemeteries, scavenging for human carrion.

Wing resembles that of a large bird of prey

BIRDS OF THUNDER

This Native American totem pole is topped with a thunderbird—a flying spirit that was believed to create thunder claps with its wing beats. The Native American people believed that the thunderbird lit up the sky with flashes of lightning from its eyes and that the individual bolts of lightning were snakes dropped from the thunderbird's beak. Most depictions of this supernatural creature have the hooked beak of an eagle—a bird that the Native Americans would have seen preying on fish, small mammals, and reptiles, such as snakes.

Horns of a stag

Dragon statue at Tianhou Temple

DRAGON POWER

This statue of a dragon is part of a temple in a large Taiwanese port and is dedicated to a sea goddess. Dragons appear in almost all cultures. They may have been inspired by fossils of giant dinosaurs unearthed by ancient people. In Western traditions, dragons are thought to be brutal beasts that eat people. However, in eastern Asia, dragons are powerful spirits that live in water and under mountains and are usually associated with good luck. One story tells how China's four biggest rivers were formed by the long bodies of dragons.

Scales of a fish

Flaming pearl is believed to bestow great powers

Claws of an eagle

Tusk is a long front tooth grown by both males and females

Skull of male narwhal

ONLY ONE HORN

A creature of myth, the unicorn is believed to be a white deer or horse with a single horn on its head. For many centuries, people thought unicorns really existed, and wealthy people collected what they believed were unicorn horns. In the Middle Ages, Danish seamen hunted whales called narwhals for their long, spiraled tusks, which often fetched huge sums as unicorn horns. Today, you could argue that the narwhal, a 1-ton mammal with a 6.5-ft- (2-m-) long, spiked tooth sticking out of its head, is even more odd-looking than a unicorn.

Record breakers

AMONG THE MILLIONS OF SPECIES that make up the animal kingdom, there a few that stand out. For example, the blue whale is the largest living animal, growing to 100 ft (30 m) in length and weighing as much as 2,500 humans. Another famous animal is the cheetah, which can outrun every other animal on land. There are, however, many lesser known extraordinary species, some of which are listed here. Biologists discover new record breakers all the time.

LARGEST ANIMAL COLONY

ARGENTINIAN ANTS
These little ants originated in South America but have spread to many other parts of the world over the last century. An 80-year-old supercolony in Europe runs for 3,730 miles (6,000 km) between Portugal and Italy.

Record: Billions of ants in a supercolony

Group: Insects

Habitat: Coast of southern Europe

FASTEST ANIMAL IN WATER

SAILFISH
This predatory fish powers through the water by rapidly sweeping its tail. It cuts through water easily with its sword-shaped bill. The sailfish raises its sail-like fin to frighten other fish into a tight ball, making them easier to hunt.

Record: Can reach a speed of 68 mph (110 kph)

Group: Ray-finned fishes

Habitat: Open oceans

LARGEST LAND INVERTEBRATE

COCONUT CRAB
Also known as the robber crab, this crustacean does not live in water but climbs on palm trees to eat fruits. Its large pincers are strong enough to crack coconuts. This species is a giant hermit crab and does not have a hard shell.

Record: Legspan of 35 in (90 cm)

Group: Crustaceans

Habitat: Tropical islands

ANIMAL LIVING IN HOTTEST HABITAT

POMPEII WORM
This sea worm lives in the Pacific Ocean, in the hot water that emerges from volcanic vents in the seabed. The worm collects chemicals in the water with its feathery gills, and bacteria in its body convert these chemicals into nutrients for the worm.

Record: Can survive at 176°F (80°C)

Group: Segmented worms

Habitat: Hydrothermal vents

SMALLEST VERTEBRATE

Head does not contain skull

AUSTRALIAN INFANTFISH
This tiny fish is the smallest animal with a backbone. It lives in muddy swamps made acidic by peat. Being really tiny, the fish can survive in just a tiny puddle of water when the swamp dries up.

Record: Length of 0.3 in (7.9 mm)

Group: Ray-finned fishes

Habitat: Peat swamps

LOUDEST ANIMAL

PISTOL SHRIMP

The pistol shrimp stuns its prey with a shock wave created by the sound of its massive pincer snapping. The sound is so loud that it creates tiny rips, or cavities, in the water that are heated to 17,850°F (9,900°C)—as hot as the Sun.

Record: Can produce sounds at 200 decibels

Group: Crustaceans

Habitat: Coral reefs

SLOWEST FISH

SEAHORSE

The seahorse can barely swim. Its fins are tiny flaps that it uses to keep itself upright. A male seahorse spends its entire adult life in the same cubic meter of water.

Record: Speed of 0.0006 mph (0.001 kph)

Group: Ray-finned fishes

Habitat: Seaweed

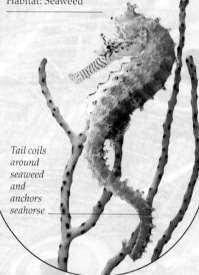

Tail coils around seaweed and anchors seahorse

FASTEST ANIMAL IN AIR

PEREGRINE FALCON

The peregrine falcon is the most widespread bird of prey in the world. It preys on other birds in midair, plummeting toward them at high speed from far above. By the time the prey sees the falcon, it is too late to get away.

Record: Can reach a speed of 200 mph (325 kph)

Group: Birds

Habitat: Cliffs

LONGEST PREGNANCY OF ANY MAMMAL

AFRICAN ELEPHANT

The scientific word for pregnancy is gestation. The African elephant has the longest gestation period of any mammal because the 220-lb (100-kg) calf must be developed enough to stand and walk soon after birth.

Record: Gestation period of 640 days

Group: Mammals

Habitat: African savanna

STRONGEST ANIMAL FOR ITS SIZE

DUNG BEETLE

Insects are capable of feats of strength that dwarf the achievements of larger animals. In 2010, researchers found that dung beetles were able to shift dung balls weighing more than 1,000 times their own weight—the equivalent of a human moving six buses at a time.

Record: Can pull 1,141 times its body weight

Group: Insects

Habitat: Grasslands and forests

LARGEST STRUCTURE FORMED BY LIVING ORGANISMS

AUSTRALIAN GREAT BARRIER REEF

Australia's Great Barrier Reef is made up of the solid remains of countless generations of coral polyps. Over a period of about 7,000 years, the structure has grown into a chain of hundreds of reefs and islands.

Record: Length of 1,615 miles (2,600 km)

Group: Cnidarians

Habitat: Warm, shallow waters

Tree of life

ALL ANIMALS ARE RELATED, some more distantly than others. Biologists are still figuring out the relationships between different species and those between larger groups of animals (phyla, classes, orders, and families). But they know enough to organize animals into a broad pattern of relationships, or tree of life. Closely related animals are clustered together. Subgroups branch off. Distantly related animals are located far from each other. This tree begins with sponges, the simplest and, perhaps, oldest type of animal. From there, other phyla branch off. The vertebrates are shown in more detail in the tree to highlight the larger and more familiar animals.

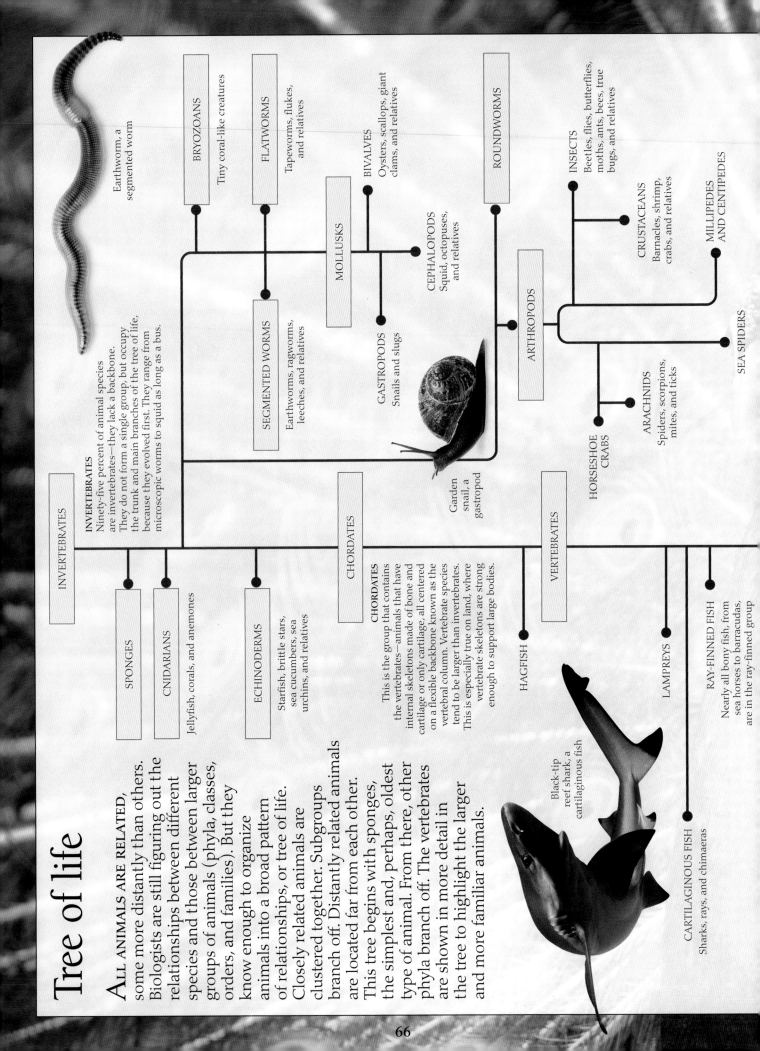

Earthworm, a segmented worm

INVERTEBRATES

INVERTEBRATES
Ninety-five percent of animal species are invertebrates—they lack a backbone. They do not form a single group, but occupy the trunk and main branches of the tree of life, because they evolved first. They range from microscopic worms to squid as long as a bus.

BRYOZOANS
Tiny coral-like creatures

FLATWORMS
Tapeworms, flukes, and relatives

MOLLUSKS

BIVALVES
Oysters, scallops, giant clams, and relatives

CEPHALOPODS
Squid, octopuses, and relatives

GASTROPODS
Snails and slugs

SEGMENTED WORMS
Earthworms, ragworms, leeches, and relatives

Garden snail, a gastropod

ROUNDWORMS

INSECTS
Beetles, flies, butterflies, moths, ants, bees, true bugs, and relatives

CRUSTACEANS
Barnacles, shrimp, crabs, and relatives

MILLIPEDES AND CENTIPEDES

ARTHROPODS

ARACHNIDS
Spiders, scorpions, mites, and ticks

SEA SPIDERS

HORSESHOE CRABS

SPONGES

CNIDARIANS
Jellyfish, corals, and anemones

ECHINODERMS
Starfish, brittle stars, sea cucumbers, sea urchins, and relatives

CHORDATES

CHORDATES
This is the group that contains the vertebrates—animals that have internal skeletons made of bone and cartilage or only cartilage, all centered on a flexible backbone known as the vertebral column. Vertebrate species tend to be larger than invertebrates. This is especially true on land, where vertebrate skeletons are strong enough to support large bodies.

VERTEBRATES

HAGFISH

LAMPREYS

RAY-FINNED FISH
Nearly all bony fish, from sea horses to barracudas, are in the ray-finned group

CARTILAGINOUS FISH
Sharks, rays, and chimaeras

Black-tip reef shark, a cartilaginous fish

66

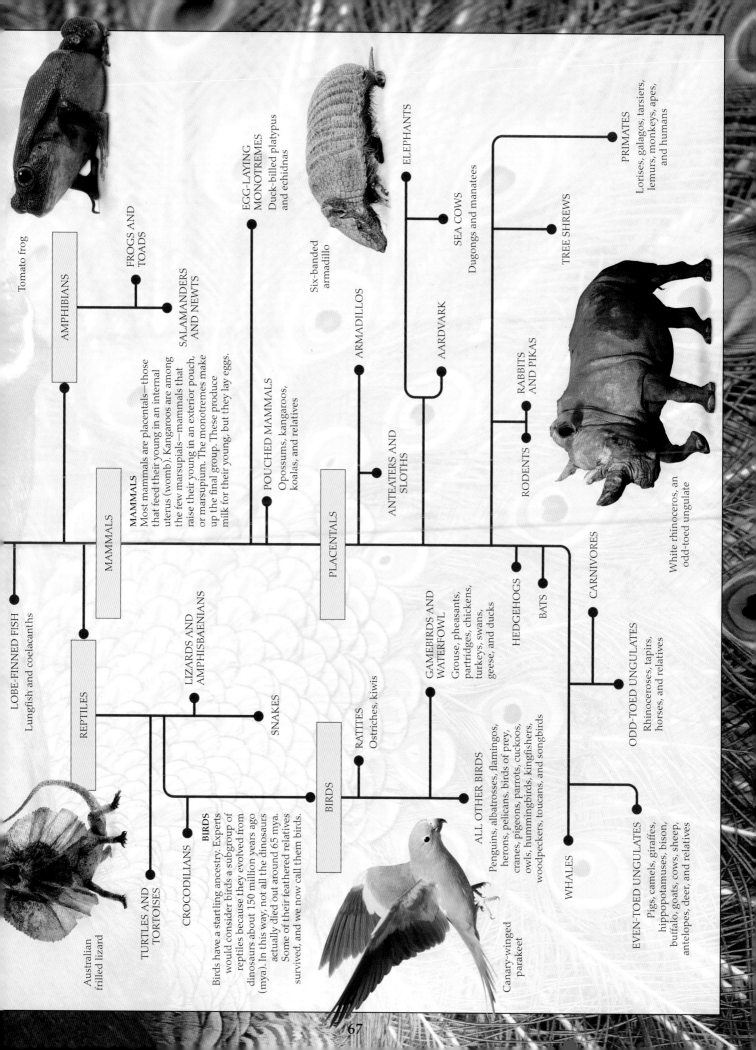

AMPHIBIANS

FROGS AND TOADS

SALAMANDERS AND NEWTS

Tomato frog

MAMMALS

MAMMALS
Most mammals are placentals—those that feed their young in an internal uterus (womb). Kangaroos are among the few marsupials—mammals that raise their young in an exterior pouch, or marsupium. The monotremes make up the final group. These produce milk for their young, but they lay eggs.

EGG-LAYING MONOTREMES
Duck-billed platypus and echidnas

POUCHED MAMMALS
Opossums, kangaroos, koalas, and relatives

Six-banded armadillo

PLACENTALS

ARMADILLOS

ANTEATERS AND SLOTHS

ELEPHANTS

AARDVARK

SEA COWS
Dugongs and manatees

TREE SHREWS

PRIMATES
Lorises, galagos, tarsiers, lemurs, monkeys, apes, and humans

RABBITS AND PIKAS

RODENTS

HEDGEHOGS

BATS

CARNIVORES

ODD-TOED UNGULATES
Rhinoceroses, tapirs, horses, and relatives

White rhinoceros, an odd-toed ungulate

LOBE-FINNED FISH
Lungfish and coelacanths

REPTILES

LIZARDS AND AMPHISBAENIANS

SNAKES

TURTLES AND TORTOISES

CROCODILIANS

Australian frilled lizard

BIRDS
Birds have a startling ancestry. Experts would consider birds a subgroup of reptiles because they evolved from dinosaurs about 150 million years ago (mya). In this way, not all the dinosaurs actually died out around 65 mya. Some of their feathered relatives survived, and we now call them birds.

BIRDS

RATITES
Ostriches, kiwis

GAMEBIRDS AND WATERFOWL
Grouse, pheasants, partridges, chickens, turkeys, swans, geese, and ducks

ALL OTHER BIRDS
Penguins, albatrosses, flamingos, herons, pelicans, birds of prey, cranes, pigeons, parrots, cuckoos, owls, hummingbirds, kingfishers, woodpeckers, toucans, and songbirds

Canary-winged parakeet

WHALES

EVEN-TOED UNGULATES
Pigs, camels, giraffes, hippopotamuses, bison, buffalo, goats, cows, sheep, antelopes, deer, and relatives

Watching animals

Blue tits are attracted to a nut-filled feeder

OBSERVING ANIMALS REQUIRES a bit of skill and a lot of patience. Getting a good look at an animal in its natural habitat can be quite difficult. Wild animals are wary of anything unusual and approaching them can be tricky—they may run away or attack if they feel scared. Spotting animals, though, can be quite rewarding—whether in the neighborhood or on a jungle safari. Knowing when and where an animal will appear is crucial to studying animals in the wild.

Magnifying glass helps study small invertebrates closely

SETTING THE SCENE
Animals are predictable and this works to a wildlife watcher's advantage. All animals need to eat and they often return to known feeding sites. For example, grizzly bears in Alaska gather near rivers in the fall to catch salmon migrating upstream. Similarly, whales and other migratory animals can be spotted traveling along their traditional routes. Wildlife enthusiasts can also attract animals, such as these blue tits, to a viewing spot by providing food or a nesting box.

This compact model saves weight on long hikes

Notebook for sketching animals is also used for recording location, time, and weather conditions of sightings

A grizzly bear catches a fish in Alaska

Binoculars offer a magnified view, allowing watchers to see details at a distance

GETTING READY
Wildlife watchers carry equipment for finding and viewing animals, recording the animals in their natural habitats, and perhaps even capturing a few. Nature lovers spend a lot of time outdoors in all kinds of weather. They need warm and dry clothing, but artificial fabrics can make high-pitched rustling sounds, which might scare away animals. So in the field, experts wear clothes made from natural material, such as cotton and wool, and in muted colors to keep from standing out.

Walking boots keep the feet warm and dry. They are comfortable on long hikes.

Sun hat keeps off the hot sun and also breaks up the tell-tale shape of the head, making it easier to hide

Large grips reduce chances of slipping in mud and on loose stones

Hide has a camouflage pattern to help it blend in with surroundings

FOLLOWING THE SEASONS

As the weather of a region changes with the seasons, so does the behavior of animals living there. A good wildlife watcher will know where a species is likely to be at each time of year. For example, they do not look for European hedgehogs in winter—as they are all hibernating—but only in summer, when the ball-shaped nests of these animals can be seen in bushes and thickets.

These common cranes have arrived in northern Europe in early summer to breed. They perform distinctive courtship displays to attract mates.

This flock of pink-footed geese is leaving Greenland in fall for Europe, where many birdwatchers travel to wetlands and estuaries to watch them arrive.

User sucks shorter tube

Flask traps insects

Pooter is a suction device for collecting tiny insects using a long, flexible tube

Insects sucked into longer tube

Large backpack holds gear, water, and food

Camera records sightings of interesting animals

Long lens can be used as a telescope to view an animal at a distance

GPS device uses satellite signals to pinpoint its exact location, telling users where they are.

Wildlife photographer spends hours inside portable hide, waiting for animals to come into view

READING THE SIGNS

Wildlife experts can find animals from the signs they leave behind. Large animals leave distinctive footprints in snow and mud, although these often disappear quickly. Trackers look for broken twigs and flattened plants that show an animal has moved in a certain direction. They keep an eye out for the signs that animals leave for each other, such as dung piles, smelly scents, and even scratches in the ground or on trees.

These marks are left by an elk, also known as a red deer, chewing on bark during winter. Fresh marks on the bark show that the elk is probably nearby.

A black bear marks its territory by gouging deep scratches in soft tree bark with its claws and teeth. The height of the mark helps in assessing how tall the bear is.

This tree has been gnawed by a beaver as it collects logs for constructing its dam. This rodent will have dug a channel nearby leading to its pool.

These holes were made by a woodpecker looking for wood-boring insects under the bark. The loud noise produced by these birds chiseling with their bills also gives away their position.

Glossary

ALGAE
Microscopic organisms that photosynthesize like a plant, but are generally single-celled. Algae often live in water or damp places.

AQUATIC
To do with water. Aquatic animals live in water or spend most of their time there.

ARTERY
A blood vessel that carries oxygen-rich blood from the heart to other body organs.

BACTERIA
Tiny, single-celled organisms that are not plant, animal, or fungus. Bacterial cells are at least 100 times smaller than an animal cell. Some bacteria cause disease, but most are harmless.

BIOLUMINESCENCE
Ability of some animals to produce light using chemicals or specialized bacteria in their bodies. Bioluminescent animals generally live in the dark—in the deep sea or in caves. The light is used to attract mates, lure prey, or startle predators.

Chameleon, an ectotherm

BLUBBER
A layer of fat under the skin that keeps sea mammals, such as whales, warm in cold water.

BRACKISH
Water that is partly salty and partly fresh. Brackish water is found in coastal swamps and river mouths where fresh water mixes with sea water.

CARBON DIOXIDE
A gas produced as a waste product by animals when they extract energy by processing sugars and other foods in their bodies. Animals take in oxygen and give out carbon dioxide when they breathe.

CARNIVORE
An animal that mostly eats meat—the flesh of other animals. Carnivores are generally predators, often killing animals that they eat.

CHITIN
A plasticlike material present in the hard body coverings of many invertebrates.

CHROMOSOME
A microscopic structure in the cells of all animals that is used as a frame around which long strands of DNA are coiled. Every species has a fixed number of chromosomes in each cell.

COLD-BLOODED
Also known as ectothermic, a cold-blooded animal is one that cannot maintain a constant body temperature. Instead, its body temperature varies with the environmental conditions.

CORPSE
The body of a dead animal.

DNA
Short for deoxyribonucleic acid, DNA is a complex chemical formed from a chain of four chemical units, or bases. The genetic code of an animal is stored in the way these four bases are ordered in its DNA chains.

DORSAL FIN
The fin on the back of an aquatic animal, such as a shark or a dolphin. The fin stops the animal from rolling as it swims.

ECTOTHERM
A cold-blooded animal. *Ecto* means "outside" and *therm* is "heat"—an ectotherm uses outside heat.

ENDOTHERM
A warm-blooded animal. *Endo* means "inside"; an endotherm uses its body heat to stay warm.

ENZYME
A protein chemical with a specific job to do in an animal's body. Digestive enzymes break up certain foods into simpler ingredients, while other enzymes copy DNA or release energy for the body to use. An enzyme's special shape helps it perform its specific task.

EVOLUTION
A process by which organisms change over a period of time and across many generations as they adapt to changes in the environment. New species are often formed in this process.

EXTINCT
A species that has died out completely.

Brown fungus growing on log

FUNGUS
An organism that is neither an animal nor a plant. A fungus, such as mushroom, grows into its food and digests it externally.

GENE
A strand of DNA that carries the instructions for a characteristic of an organism—such as the color of a bird's feathers or the shape of its wings.

GILL
The organ used by many aquatic animals to absorb oxygen from water and give out carbon dioxide. On land, this function is performed by lungs in many vertebrates.

GIZZARD
A muscular part of a bird's gut used to grind food.

HABITAT
The place where an animal lives.

Toucan's bill contains keratin

HERBIVORE
An animal that only eats plant food. It may eat leaves (folivore), fruits (frugivore), seed (granivore), sap and juices (exudivore), or roots (radicivore).

HERMAPHRODITE
An animal that has both male and female sex organs. Some hermaphrodites start life as one sex and change into the other as they grow. Other hermaphrodites have both sets of sex organs at the same time.

HYBRID
A cross between two species or breeds. A mule is a hybrid of a horse and a donkey, while a mongrel is a hybrid between dog breeds.

INSULATOR
A substance that stops heat from escaping from an animal's body, keeping it warm. Blubber, feathers, and hair are the common insulators found in animals.

INVERTEBRATE
Any animal that is not a member of the phylum Chordata. Most of the world's animals are invertebrates, including insects, spiders, worms, mollusks, and crustaceans.

Clownfish, a hermaphrodite that changes from male to female as it grows

KERATIN
A flexible protein present in the external body features of vertebrates, such as hair, feathers, claws, scales, horn sheaths, and fingernails.

KLEPTOPARASITE
An animal that survives by stealing food from another hunter, generally of a different species.

LANDLOCKED
Surrounded by land on all sides.

LARVA
The young form of an insect or other invertebrate that looks different from the adult form and also lives in a different way. A caterpillar is an example of a larva.

LIFT FORCE
The force that pushes a flying animal off the ground.

MEMBRANE
A thin layer or barrier that may allow some substances to pass through.

MICROSCOPIC
When something is too small to see with the naked eye. A microscope is used to observe it.

NUTRIENTS
The useful parts of food, such as sugars, proteins, fats, oils, vitamins, and minerals. An animal's digestive system extracts these from food.

NYMPH
An early stage of development of an insect or other invertebrate that generally looks and lives in the same way as the organism's adult form.

OSMOSIS
A process that makes water move in and out of animals' bodies. The movement takes place from water that is less salty to water that is more salty. Sea animals lose water while freshwater animals absorb it.

OXYGEN
A substance used by an animal's body in chemical reactions that release energy from sugars and other foods. It is taken in by breathing in air or absorbing it from water.

PARASITE
An animal that lives on or in another animal of a different species. The parasite weakens its host but does not kill it.

Diving beetle nymph underwater

PHYLUM
The largest grouping used to organize, or classify, life-forms within the animal kingdom. There are dozens of animal phyla. Some of the main ones are Arthropoda (insects and crabs), Mollusca (snails and squid), and Chordata (vertebrates).

PIGMENTS
Chemicals that give color to an organism. Giving color may be the main function of the pigment or the coloration may be incidental. For example, the pigments in the eye are used as light detectors.

PREDATOR
An animal that hunts and kills other animals for food.

PROTEIN
A complex chemical found in all life-forms but most prominently in animals. Proteins help build body parts. Enzymes are examples of proteins.

SALIVA
The liquid produced by salivary glands in the mouth of an animal to moisten food, making it easier to swallow and digest.

SCUTE
An armored plate of bone covered in skin or horny keratin. A turtle shell is made up of interlocking scutes while a crocodile's body is protected by ridges of scutes.

SPECIES
A group of animals that look the same and live in the same way and are also able to breed with each other to produce fertile offspring that will be able to reproduce themselves.

Turtle shell contains scutes

SYMBIOSIS
A partnership between two animals of different species that live with each other. In most cases, each animal provides a service or benefit to the other in the relationship.

TERRITORY
An area of land or water defended by an animal. Territory is used as a feeding space or as an area for mates to live and unwanted members of the same species are driven away.

TETRAPOD
A vertebrate with four limbs.

TRACHEA
The scientific name for a windpipe through which humans—and other tetrapods—breathe. However, insects and other invertebrates also have dozens of air tubes, also called trachea, which allow air into all parts of the body.

URINE
The liquid waste of mammals and other animals. While dung, or feces, is the undigested materials in food, urine is the waste removed from the blood and body tissues.

VEIN
A blood vessel that carries oxygen-poor blood from the body organs toward the heart.

VENOM
Poison that is produced by an animal and injected into another by a bite, scratch, or sting. Venom is used in hunting as well as in defense.

VERTEBRATE
An animal with a backbone—a set of small vertebrae that connect to form a flexible spine. The vertebrate groups are fish, amphibians, reptiles, birds, and mammals.

WARM-BLOODED
Also known as endothermic, a warm-blooded animal is one that controls its body temperature internally, using a lot of energy to heat or cool its body, so it stays at more or less the same temperature whatever the weather conditions at that time.

Leopard, a predator, with its kill

Index

Acknowledgments

Dorling Kindersley would like to thank: Caitlin
Doyle for proofreading; Dr. Laurence Errington for
the index; and Aanchal Awasthi, Honlung Zach
Ragui, and Nitu Singh for design assistance.

The publishers would also like to thank the
following for their kind permission to reproduce
their photographs:

(Key: a-above; b-below/bottom; c-center; f-far; l-left;
r-right; t-top)

Alamy Images: Amazon-Images 23tr, CML Images
59br, Mark Conlin / VWPICS / Visual&Written SL
42bl, Stephen Dalton / Photoshot Holdings Ltd 39tr,
Chris Mattison 32tr, Mauritius images GmbH 32b,
MicroScan / Phototake Inc. 12br, Todd Mintz 42crb,
Mira 26tl, Richard Mittleman / Gon2Foto 11br, V.
Muthuraman / SuperStock 36clb, NaturePics 43cra,
Matthew Oldfield 24br, Clément Philippe / Arterra
Picture Library 69crb, Bjorn Svensson / Science Photo
Library 69br, Duncan Usher 48-49bc, Dave Watts
13cr, 17ca; Ardea: Steve Downer 27bl, Ferrero-Labat
22-23c, François Gohier 48bl, Stefan Meyers 30cra;
Corbis: Hinrich Baesemann / DPA 30-31b, Hal Beral
9tr, Carolina Biological / Visuals Unlimited 10cla,
Nigel Cattlin / Visuals Unlimited 15clb, Ralph
Clevenger 42-43, Dr John D. Cunningham / Visuals
Unlimited 69cr, Mark Downey 2bc, 24tl, Macduff
Everton 53cla, Michael & Patricia Fogden 18-19, 36bl,
Stephen Frink 10b, Tim Graham 68br, James Hager /
Robert Harding World Imagery 23c, Dave Hamman /
Gallo Images 55crb, Martin Harvey 37br, Martin
Harvey / Gallo Images 22bl, Eric & David Hosking
4tl, 48cl, Jason Isley - Scubazoo / Science Faction

42cl, Wolfgang Kaehler 28br, Karen Kasmauski /
Science Faction 61tr, Thomas Kitchin & Victoria
Hurst / First Light 13br, Peter Kneffel / DPA 54tl,
Stephen J. Krasemann / All Canada Photos 34tl, Frans
Lanting 4bl, 31cl, 33br, 60bc, Frans Lemmens 49cra,
Wayne Lynch / All Canada Photos 31cb, John E.
Marriott / All Canada Photos 31tr, Dan McCoy -
Rainbow / Science Faction 50cla, Joe McDonald
11clb, 38cl, 68cl, Tim Mckulka / UNMIS / Reuters
52-53, Dong Naide / Xinhua Press 53tr, David A.
Northcott 6tl, Michael Redmer / Visuals Unlimited
6bc (plethodon jordani), 9tl, Bryan Reynolds /
Science Faction 59fcra, David Scharf / Science Faction
55cl, Shoot 60t, David Spears / Clouds Hill Imaging
Ltd. 65tc, Keren Su 55tl, Jeff Vanuga 58t, Carlos
Villoch / Specialist Stock 26-27, Visuals Unlimited
7br, 44tl, Stuart Westmorland 8clb, 11tr, Ralph White
62bl, Lawson Wood 27br, Norbert Wu / Science
Faction 20bl, 47c; Dorling Kindersley: ESPL -
modelmaker 50r, Exmoor Zoo, Devon 15cra (Azara's
Agouti), Hunterian Museum (University of Glasgow)
4cr, 17tr, Trustees of the National Museums Of
Scotland 17cla, Natural History Museum, London 4br
(larger cockroach), 8tr, 12fbr, 13tl, 16cra, 44br, 58br
(two larger coackroaches), 58fcrb (larger cockroach),
59c (larger cockroach), 68ftr, Based on a photo by
David Robinson / The Open University 33cr, Rough
Guides 50bl, 51br, 61crb, Stanley Park, Totem Park,
Vancouver, British Columbia 2l, 63r, University
College, London 51l, Whipsnade Zoo, Bedfordshire
Barrie Watts 66ca, 67cra, Jerry Young 4tr, 4cra,
10-11tc, 24cra, 37ca, 56cla, 67tl; FLPA: Ingo Arndt /
Minden Pictures 37tr, Flip De Nooyer / Minden 68bc,
Michael Durham / Minden Pictures 19cra (leeches),

Suzi Eszterhas / Minden Pictures 47br, John Holmes
30-31tc, Donald M. Jones / Minden Pictures 69cra,
Mark Moffett / Minden Pictures 29tr, Jurgen &
Christine Sohns 35tr, Konrad Wothe / Minden
Pictures 45cra, 65cla, Norbert Wu / Minden Pictures
47clb; Fotolia: Eric Isselee 60cl; Getty Images: AFP
64bl, Gerry Bishop / Visuals Unlimited 46br, Tom
Brakefield - The Stock Connection / Science Faction
15br, The Bridgeman Art Library 57cr, Stephen
Dalton / Minden Pictures 29br, George Day / Gallo
Images 8tl, David Doubilet / National Geographic
8-9bc, Georgette Douwma / Photographer's Choice
27tr, Richard du Toit / Gallo Images 47tr, Guy
Edwardes / The Image Bank 59tl, Eurasia / Robert
Harding World Imagery 62-63bc, George Grall /
National Geographic 18clb, Louis-Laurent
Grandadam / The Image Bank 55b, Jamie Grill 69ca,
Henry Guttmann / Hulton Archive 15tl, Hulton
Archive 59bl, David Maitland 44cra, Joe McDonald /
Visuals Unlimited 46-47, Bruno Morandi / The Image
Bank 20tl, Marwan Naamani / AFP 33tr, Piotr
Naskrecki / Minden Pictures 33cla, Iztok Noc /
Photodisc 56-57, Radius Images 65br, 71cra, David
Silverman 23br, Keren Su 7tr, U.S. Navy 54bl, Mario
Vazquez / AFP 43tr, Gary Vestal / Photographer's
Choice 7l, 25b, Alex Wild / Visuals Unlimited, Inc.
65cb; imagequestmarine.com: 64br; NASA: GSFC
/ Craig Mayhew & Robert Simmon 51t; naturepl.
com: Chris Gomersall 41tc, Rolf Nussbaumer 45i,
Andy Rouse 36r, Kim Taylor 25tr, 38b (dragonflies),
Dave Watts 40tc, 40tr, Wild Wonders of Europe /
Rautiainen 69bl; Photolibrary: Kathie Atkinson /
Oxford Scientific (OSF) 40clb, Stefan Auth /
Imagebroker.net 54br, Paulo de Oliveira / Oxford

Scientific (OSF) 10cra, 62cla, David B. Fleetham /
Oxford Scientific (OSF) 27cr, François Gilson / Bios
40bl, jspix jspix / Imagebroker.net 12tr, Steven
Kazlowski / Alaskastock 60-61c, Morales Morales /
Age fotostock 64clb, Rolf Nussbaumer / Imagebroker.
net 21clb, Frank Parker / Age fotostock 35 (main
image), Jean-Paul Chatagnon / Bios 49tr, Gerhard
Schultz / Oxford Scientific (OSF) 40crb, Gerhard
Schulz / Bios 41crb, M. Varesvuo 20-21tc; Science
Photo Library: Susumu Nishinaga 12bc, Power &
Syred 29tl, 46r, D. Roberts 39br, Volker Steger 21crb,
21fcrb; SuperStock: Minden Pictures 33cla.

Wall Chart images: Corbis: Peter Kneffel / DPA (crb/
rescue dog), Frans Lanting (cra/penguin), Norbert Wu
/ Science Faction (crb/spotted shrimp goby); Dorling
Kindersley: Natural History Museum, London (br/
larger cockroach); Getty Images: Georgette Douwma
/ Photographer's Choice (fcra/fish), Gary Vestal /
Photographer's Choice (c); Photolibrary: jspix jspix /
Imagebroker.net (tl/macaw).

Jacket images: Front: Dorling Kindersley: Natural
History Museum, London ca/ (butterfly); Getty
Images: WIN-Initiative (main image); Back:
Photolibrary: Watt Jim / Pacific Stock bl, jspix /
Imagebroker.net c.

All other images © Dorling Kindersley
For further information see: www.dkimages.com